GLASS CRAFT
Designing · Forming · Decorating

GLASS

Designing · Forming · Decorating

CRAFT

KAY KINNEY

CHILTON BOOK COMPANY

PHILADELPHIA NEW YORK LONDON

Copyright © 1962 by Kay Kinney

First Edition   748

Second Printing, June 1963
Third Printing, December 1965
Fourth Printing, May 1967
Fifth Printing, July 1971

All Rights Reserved

Published in Philadelphia by Chilton Book Company,
and simultaneously in Ontario, Canada,
by Thomas Nelson & Sons, Ltd.

Designed by William E. Lickfield

ISBN   0-8019-0624-5
Library of Congress Catalog Card Number 61–14025

Manufactured in the United States of America

FOR MY HUSBAND AND MY SON

without whose patience and understanding this book could not have been written

The author wishes to express deep gratitude to the following persons for their suggestions, and often their corroborative evaluations, and most of all for their unfailing friendship:

MRS. ALTA ANDRE
MRS. LAMBERT CRAEMER
MRS. EDITH BAHN D'ELISCU
MR. MARTIN HANSON
MRS. CARROLL HARE
MRS. CARL KILTS
MRS. ANTHONY ULM
MRS. SHIRLEY WILSON

CONTENTS

GLASS CRAFT
Designing · Forming · Decorating

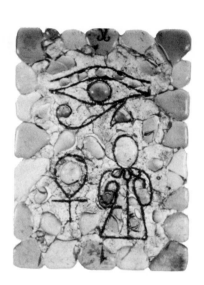

A. INTRODUCTORY

HISTORICAL

To Pliny, the ancient natural historian, is attributed the first recorded description of the source of glass. His romantic legend of accidental discovery prevails: that a ship, laden with natron, was moored at the mouth of the river Belus; the crew, while preparing their food on the shore, rested their cooking utensils on blocks of the natron. The heat from the fire caused the natron to melt and form a flux that reduced the sand to glass. There is considerable disagreement as to whether glass formation, as we know it, could have been produced in this simple manner, some experts declaring that undoubtedly the chemicals found in the river had a definite bearing on the composition; others, that natron was probably of a different nature than the present definition implies.

Whether the legend is based on fact or fiction, all commentators seem to agree that the origin of glass must have been accidental, and that such origin dates to at least 1500 B.C., for certain Egyptian tombs contain incised portrayals of glass blowers at work. There are disputes as to how the art of glass blowing spread to Europe, but it seems logical that methods were brought by Romans, as Biblical references place the Romans in Egypt as oppressors.

It is a certainty that glass blowing was perfected in Italy, flourishing there during medieval times, and indeed, the secrets of that era have passed from father to son in many families, so that today examples of the finest workmanship are still being produced.

FUNDAMENTAL COMPOSITION OF GLASS

"Glassmaking of today is a new art, because but perhaps a century and a half have elapsed since it began to emerge from the almost total eclipse it experienced during the dark ages, and to the nineteenth century must be assigned nearly all the improvements which have placed it once again among the arts. Still, the ancients were familiar with many processes which we consider new; many of our improvements of today are simply lost processes rediscovered. As a whole, the constituents, their proportions, methods of aggregation and association, and the manipulation of glass, are along the same general lines that guided the ancients; and we have been but regaining that which has been buried beneath the dust of centuries." (Quotation from *Elements of Glass and Glass Making*, by Benjamin F. Biser, Glass and Pottery Publishing Co., Pittsburgh, Pa.)

The title "glass" is applied to such a perplexing variety of substances, both chemically and commercially, that it makes an exact definition difficult. Differentiating between the forms of silicon, the alkalies, and the oxides would prove confusing to any

but the technical engineer. There are textbooks available in university and other libraries, which give detailed and exhaustive data on countless formulations.

Generally speaking, glass consists of silica, alkali, and some other base such as lime or lead oxide. Metallic oxides are used for coloring glass batches. While I realize that this is probably oversimplification, mention of possible substitutions would cause ramifications that would change the purpose of this book entirely. Since the techniques described within these pages deal with some finished form of glass, re-employed as a raw material, it seems feasible to begin with the premise that any names used apply to such finished forms.

MODERN PROCESSING OF GLASS

The two primary functions of glass are the transmission of light, and imperviousness to moisture. For centuries, glass has proved to be the most effective material for windows from both standpoints. There has yet to be found a superior substitute for the glass vessel or container, for even acids, with the exception of hydrofluoric, do not affect its surfaces.

The basic principles of the old processes still exist. Even the tools employed in glass blowing are much the same. Although commercial containers are no longer blown individually, and modern machinery has increased the output, the principle remains the same, for the machine merely duplicates the procedure of blowing. Machinery has also speeded up the manufacture of sheet glass, but the fact remains that the glass must still start with the molten batch and be rolled into sheet form, albeit more efficiently.

The following quotation is from *General Chemistry,* by Young and Porter, Prentice-Hall, Inc., 1958:

"*Plate glass* is made by pouring the molten silicate mixture on a large iron plate. It flows over the smooth iron surface, forming an even layer. To insure uniform thickness, it is rolled with heavy, hot iron rollers which travel on adjustable guides at the edges of the iron plate or casting table. After it has been rolled, the glass is placed in an annealing furnace, where it is cooled very slowly. Glass that has been cooled quickly is brittle and breaks easily. Slow cooling (annealing) gives the molecules a chance to arrange themselves in the plastic mass in such a way as to avoid internal strain. The surface of the glass is made perfectly smooth by grinding it first with iron rubbers and sand, then with leather-covered rubbers and fine emery dust. In many cases of grinding and polishing, the finished product is not much more than half as thick as the original plate.

"*Window glass* is made by rolling the plastic material into thin sheets. In some factories window glass is made by blowing the molten glass with a blowpipe which is connected with a tank of compressed air. The pipe is withdrawn slowly while a carefully regulated flow of air is maintained. By this means the glass is blown into a cylinder several feet long. The cylinder is then detached from the blowpipe and cut lengthwise with a diamond cutter. It is placed on a flat surface in a furnace, with the cut side up, and heated until it softens and the cylinder slowly opens and flattens out. It is then annealed and finally cut into sheets of desired sizes."

The following quotation is from *Modern Chemistry,* by Dull-Brooks-Metcalfe, Henry Holt & Co., 1954:

"*The Working of Glass.* In making hand-blown glass, the glassblower inserts one end of a six-foot-long blowpipe into a pot of molten glass. He rolls the blowpipe around until the required amount of glass has adhered to the end of the pipe. Then he blows a bubble in the glass and fashions it into the desired shape. Frequently he blows the bubble into a mold to give the object its finished form. However, the skill of the experienced glassblower in making water goblets and other objects, without the aid of a mold, is great. He uses a few simple tools, such as a paddle and a rounded rod to shape the article. The surplus glass is cut off by shears while it is still plastic. Laboratory glassware and the better grades of table glass are still made by the hand-blown process.

"*Window glass* is made by lowering a horizontal rod into the molten glass in a furnace. As the rod is drawn vertically upward, the glass clings to the rod and forms a sheet. The thickness of the sheet of glass can be regulated by controlling the rate at which the glass is elevated, and also by controlling the temperature of the molten glass in the furnace."

After thoughtful consideration of the brief description of commercial glass manufacture, it becomes evident that such processing is out of the question for the average individual. Therefore, sheet glass and certain other glass forms, end products as far as their original manufacture is concerned, have been regarded as raw materials for the techniques, since physical manipulation, decorating, and firing procedures completely alter their appearance.

A technique is a manner or method of handling details in the execution of an undertaking. A project is the specific undertaking itself, and may employ a single technique or a combination of separate techniques. Techniques as outlined in these pages are based on the action or reaction of the materials listed; on thermal and chemical factors which would influence a particular material, phase, or final completion of a project.

Techniques pertaining to glass in sheet form are for the most part manual, requiring dexterity to some degree. Decorating techniques involve not only manipulation of tools, but an understanding of the characteristics of the decorating media. It is the specific project which determines selection of techniques, and ultimate success depends on your personal judgment.

Where basic techniques have previously been outlined, only references will be given in later chapters. In some instances, I thought it desirable to rely on sequence photos rather than detailed description, to clarify a technique.

I sincerely hope that you will find working with glass as exciting as I have, and that these pages will be a stimulus for future experiments of great scope.

B. BASIC TECHNIQUES OF SHEET GLASS

TOOLS AND EQUIPMENT

Fig. 1. An enameling kiln. This model has stepless power control for temperature regulation.

Fig. 2. An enameling kiln with a pyrometer. Pyrometers are usually extra equipment. They can be installed in any kiln.

Fig. 3. A ceramic electric kiln, 2⅔ cubic foot capacity.

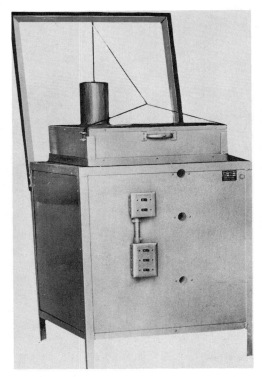

Fig. 4. A high-fire electric kiln, 8 cubic foot capacity, with a counter-weighted lid.

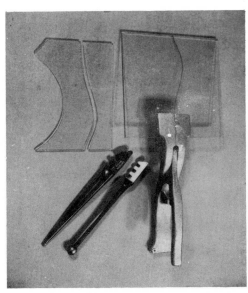

Fig. 5. Three glass hand cutters. The slender model at the left is capable of scoring small, intricate curves, and has a carbide cutting wheel. The center cutter is a standard model and has a ball end for tapping. The large tool is a tile breaker, with a cutting wheel located at the right corner of the lower "handle." The scorings are aligned with grooves on either side of the small hole in the upper jaw; severance of single or double curves is executed by merely compressing the two handles at the edge of the glass blank.

8

Fig. 6. This gauge cutter scores the inside of bottle necks or tubes. The cutting wheel is located at the end of the metal rod. The clamp can be adjusted to position the wheel at the desired depth. A V-shaped bar is mounted on a parallel rod for outside positioning. The tool is of scissor construction.

Fig. 7. An "egg beater" hand drill, with spade-type drill bits.

Fig. 9. A bench grinder with adjustable safety glass shields. The left wheel is a coarse rubber abrasive for grinding extremely rough edges; at the right, a fine rubber abrasive wheel polishes minor irregularities.

Fig. 8. A drill press (table model). The upright arm controls raising or lowering of the chuck and drill bits. No clamps or jigs are needed, due to precise engineering. The speed of the drill is controlled by adjusting the pulleys and the belt.

Fig. 10. A propane torch may be used for quick annealing of copper wire.

Fig. 11. An electric table broiler may be used to heat segments of glass prior to crushing. The hot glass is removed with tongs and dropped into a pan of cold water. A network of small fractures results, thus facilitating the crushing of the glass by hand.

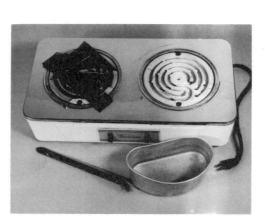

Fig. 12. An electric hot plate can be substituted for the broiler.

Fig. 13. Annealed glass is placed in a skillet and crushed with a hammer. The double-headed hammer shown is a type used by automotive repair shops for body and fender work.

Fig. 14. A kitchen waste disposal unit pulverizes glass; no water is used. The unit is virtually noiseless and need not be mounted.

Fig. 15. A hand sprayer for applying glass glaze or mold separator. Compression is provided by a replaceable cylinder.

Fig. 16. A wire record rack holds small pieces of glass upright for instant identification and selection.

SELECTING SHEET GLASS

Before proceeding with the main theme of this book—the fusion of glass—it is necessary to evaluate the various types of sheet glass. In this diverse field, materials which are designed for far different purposes are used; sheet glass is manufactured specifically for windows, doors, desks, table tops, etc. Production requirements involve factors of strength, surface quality, durability, and clarity. The manufacturer understandably is concerned only with the best (or at least satisfactory) finished products for these purposes. It is certain that the composition of glass differs, and because of these differences understanding of the characteristics of sheet glass becomes essential. Reapplication of heat, addition of colorants or unrelated materials with a greater or lesser coefficient, age or weathering of used glass, all present problems, and although not necessarily insoluble, these problems must be calculated in the successful fusing of glass.

Each type of glass has individual traits, which cause actions and often reactions in a predictable manner. Any attempt to coerce or change what has proved to be a set behavior pattern is futile. So it is necessary that the glass craftsman know the charcteristics of all types of sheet glass. There are many brands available. Unknown or unrecommended glass should always be tested in the particular kiln which will be regularly used before any major project is attempted.

We must assume that there is much experimental work to be done before we can predict exactly what to expect when the kiln is finally cool and the finished glass piece removed. Most flat or sheet glass can be fired successfully, but due to the functional differences of the various types of glass, the fusion temperature is apt to be unknown. Plate glass, for instance, may be extremely hard, especially that which is used for store windows, since it must be able to withstand pressure from people as well as from extremes of cold or heat. Glass salesmen ordinarily do not know the fusion temperature of the particular brands they sell, but they are usually co-operative about furnishing scrap samples of various types of glass, which can be tested for heat and for reaction to color. Some brands of window glass are extremely tough and in most cases the glass is also brittle, often splitting when irregular shapes are cut. Such glass may require a high firing temperature.

The following is a list of types (not brands) of glass, which may be helpful:

Picture Glass

Extremely thin—to minimize the weight of framed pictures. Excellent for jewelry, Christmas ornaments, any project where weight must be considered. Fairly hard glass, to compensate for the lack of thickness. Tendency to be brittle. Fusing approximates that of single-strength glass.

Window Glass—Single Strength

Fairly light weight. For medium-sized jewelry, small panels, mobiles, or bent forms. Two thicknesses for lamination (that is, colorant or other decorating media contained between two sheets of glass). Two sheets of single-strength glass, when fused together, are durable enough for larger projects, and have the added advantage of sealing in materials which would otherwise peel from the surface.

Window Glass—Double Strength

Thicker glass for larger projects. Used as a single sheet, this provides the right thickness for pieces up to six inches. Lamination of double-strength glass equals ¼ inch in thickness, and makes the finished piece strong enough for larger projects.

Textured Glass

Most brands fire to total transparency. Has advantage of progressive thicknesses from ⅛ inch up, for increasingly larger projects.

Crystal

Obtainable in thicknesses as above. Advantage of excellent quality, with a minimum of impurities. Easy to cut;

Fig. 17. Two trays. ³⁄₁₆″ solar gray glass was used. Solar glass is manufactured to reduce glare in industrial and institutional buildings.

responds to medium firing. More expensive than window glass.

Plate Glass

Has tendency to separate irregularly in cutting, unless professional equipment is available. Expensive to purchase. Most varieties fire successfully at varying temperatures.

Industrial Glass

Usually hard, brittle glass. Available in blue, gray, black, yellow, or green, for light filtration. Medium firing range.

Summary

As a rule, sheet glass with green to yellowish edges is fairly easy to cut, and fire within a medium temperature range. This is considered medium firing glass. Colorless edges usually indicate hard, brittle glass, inclined to split, requiring more heat. Definite turquoise edges often denote a type of glass that dulls or frosts unless a flux or flux colorant is added.

The above listing is of colorless sheet glass (with the exception of tinted industrial glass), and was selected for basic procedures of sheet glass, because slight variations can be controlled by simple adjustments in cutting and firing. Stained (cathedral) glass requires different techniques, and is dealt with in another section, "Miscellaneous Glass."

Basic Tools

Hand cutter, preferably with a ball tip.

Lubricant for the cutter: ½ kerosene, ½ light oil.

Padding: ¼ inch sheet cork, or firm carpeting.

Glass cleaner: denatured alcohol, or detergent.

Clean rags.

Abrasive stone.

Wide-jawed pliers.

Graphite glass pencils.

Optional Tools

Tile or end-wire cutters.

Rubber abrasive wheels (if an electrically operated bench grinder is available).

"Eggbeater" hand drill, electric drill or drill press, for drilling holes.

Circle cutters.

Lens cutters.

CUTTING PATTERNS

As with other crafts, a pattern for cutting glass is desirable, especially where exact dimensions must be followed, for it is almost impossible to gauge measurements visually. Because of the complete transparency of the glass, even a smudge or speck of dust on the worktable is distracting, and often causes an unconscious deviation from the intended straight line or curve.

Surface sketching is most easily done with a graphite pencil for glass and metal. Such pencils mark the glossy surface with a fine clear line, and they may be sharpened in a pencil sharpener. The glass must be dry, and free of oil or dust. After cutting, you can erase any traces of the pencil line with a damp cloth.

If the shape is to be duplicated, a pattern should be sketched on paper or stencil paper. This permanent pattern can be cellophane-taped to the underside, or subsurface, of the glass, and can serve as a guide for cutting if the glass is thin enough to follow the design accurately. Thick glass presents some problem of parallax, distorting the pattern with each change of vision. In this case, you can trace the design from the permanent pattern on the surface with a graphite glass pencil.

So-called grease pencils and felt-tipped pens are also effective for marking glass, but as the markings are quite broad, they are apt to be inaccurate.

Designing the Pattern

There are only three basic cuts which can be successfully separated from a panel of glass. These are the straight line, the single arc, and the double or S curve. Acute angles should be avoided in planning the design, for two straight or curved lines meeting at an angle which will ultimately form an *inner* cutout portion, inevitably continue their directed paths at the junction, thereby splitting the shape into three or more sections. Outer or protruding angles, of course, can be used, since the divergent lines merely continue past the shape, usually to the outer edge of the glass panel. The design can be altered a little to change the inner acute angle into a variation of the S curve, without damaging the original concept. Stained glass church windows illustrate this principle perfectly; where acute angles occur, separate sections of glass have been cut, and sharp angles are delineated only by the leading.

CUTTING THE GLASS

The phrase "glass cutting" is misleading, for no one can actually cut glass (the accepted definition of the word "cut" being "to sever") manually. Glass can be sawed with professional equipment, but in this case the severance is accomplished by a machine, and not by the strength of the operator.

It is the nature of sheet glass to react to the incising of its surface with cleavage or fracture, usually from the subsurface. The intention in cutting is to control and guide such fracture to a predetermined shape. Thus, the craftsman is using a basic principle to create his own form. The procedure is as follows:

(A) A line is scored on the surface of the glass.

(B) The glass is turned over and pressure is applied directly over the scoring, resulting in the severance, or cutting of the glass.

Since sheet glass is brittle, the table top or other working area should be level and unwarped, for an uneven working surface causes intermittent pressure of the cutter. To cushion the inflexible glass from the rigid working surface, padding of some sort is necessary. Sheet cork, firm carpeting, or even a half-inch layer of newspaper provides enough resiliency. The glass is placed on the padding, and the cutting is done directly over the glass. You should be standing while you do this work.

As with other operations dependent on the natural aptitude or physical habit patterns of the craftsman, there is no "only" way to manipulate the cutter. Some professionals grasp the cutter in a fist hold, which places the thumb on top of the ball end; others slant the cutter parallel with the glass, the index finger being placed near the cutting wheel. Holding the cutter as though it were a pencil is a universal favorite. Whatever position seems natural to you is certainly the one to use.

The tiny wheel inserted in the end of the cutter rotates on a minute shaft, and it is this wheel which scores a straight or curved line. Even and continuous pressure of the cutter is essential as the wheel rotates, for each stop or start realigns the cutter slightly, resulting in an irregular cut. It is the general (and entirely reasonable) assumption of the novice that extreme pressure must be applied. Usually such pressure splits the panel of glass. A broad and fuzzy white scoring identifies too much pressure. On the other hand, too light a pressure will not incise the glass sufficiently to ensure cleavage. The angle of the cutter itself plays an important part in successful cutting: unless the wheel rotates in a vertical position, the cleavage will slant at whatever angle the wheel has been directed.

Until the mechanics of glass cutting become so automatic that you need not plan each step, it would be well to analyze procedure. In following the pattern, it is important to gauge correctly the ultimate directional sweep of the cutter. This can only be determined if the unscored portion of the design is visible. In making a scored line from the top to the bottom of a panel your hand is placed over the directional path of the pattern. Thus it is logical to start at the bottom, and move toward the top in order to begin any deviation before abrupt directional change is necessary. Depending on the curves indicated, a right-handed person may find his pattern momentarily obscured if he scores on the right portion of the design; working from the bottom, but on the left side, makes it possible to see the pattern at all times. While it is true that most professional cutters of window and door panels score from top to bottom of the glass sheet to be severed, it must be remembered that only straight lines are required, and that a straight-edge, T-square, or ruler provides a guide for the cutter, so that the operator need not even look at the cutter during its progress.

Allowing for the Margin

Even with a simple straight scored line, separation from the main panel of glass is impossible unless there is sufficient leverage to remove the excess glass. For this reason, a minimum of ½" margin surrounding any shape must be allowed in selecting the panel from which the shape is to be cut. Thus, if the shape is 6" wide and 8" long, the panel should be not smaller than 7" by 9". Only in the case of rectangles or squares which are to be cut from perfectly true-edged panels can this allowance be eliminated; provided that at least one existing dimension of the rectangle or square may be measured merely from the edge.

The sweep of the free-hand score line should never be calculated past the point where control in following the pattern can be maintained. In describing an outer arc, there is always a tendency to slant the cutter toward the design, resulting in an undercut separation of the shape. Inner arcs produce the reverse, or slanting projections from the outline. Therefore, a free-form shape should be scored in sections. How the design is divided depends solely on how far you can propel the cutter in a true vertical position. Usually the unit of padding, pattern, and glass is placed in such a position that you can predetermine stopping points. Upon reaching such a point, lift the cutter, turn the unit so that resumption of the pattern can continue to the next calculated sweep of the cutter, and pick up the path of the scored line with the cutter, just behind the previous termination. Each interruption of the cutting will result in a tiny protuberance; if stopping points are planned on outer arcs, they can be removed easily with a carborundum stone.

Separating the Shape from the Glass Panel

After the outline of the shape has been scored, turn the panel over, face down on the padding. It is at this juncture that the actual cleavage (or "cutting") takes place. If the glass is double strength or thinner, press the thumb firmly over the scored line to fracture the glass. For heavier glass, tap with the ball end of the cutter; short, light blows produce a cleaner separation than hard pounding. Once the fracture starts, it may be necessary to follow the entire outline until complete cleavage is attained.

The shape, although cut, is still held to the original panel because of the various curves. To separate it, again turn the panel over, and score additional lines, beginning approximately ⅛″ from the cut shape, and radiating toward the edge of the panel. Tap these in turn on the reverse side. The new fractures stop at the cleaved line of the shape, and the margin can be removed in sections.

Once scored, the margins should be removed at once, for in some cases the scored line will have a tendency to heal itself.

Circular Cutting

Although it is possible, with practice, to approximate the perfectly round shape, there can never be measurements as exact as are demanded by certain fields such as architectural projects where blueprints must be followed. There are mechanical devices which have been designed for this purpose. A rod or bar pivots from a small metal base, the cutting wheel being mounted vertically in the outer end of the bar. You need know only the diameter of the circle, for the bar is scaled in diameter readings, eliminating the need for a preliminary pattern. Adjust the bar to the desired measurement; it is held firmly by a small set-screw. Set the base in the center of the glass panel, and hold it securely with one thumb while sweeping the outer end of the bar in a complete circle with the other hand. If you begin the scoring under the arm which is holding the center base, you can complete the circle without stopping the cutter. To cleave the shape and remove the margins, follow procedure as outlined for hand cutting. Circles from 3″ to 24″ may be scored with this type of cutter.

For smaller disks, ranging from ½″ to 5″, a lens cutter may be employed. Diminutive circles prohibit the use of a center base, and these cutters are designed on a slightly different principle. The adjustable center bar and rod pivot from a stand which is mounted on a wooden platform. Equipped with a spring, you can operate the hand knob entirely above the glass. This principle is also used in larger professional equipment. (See Figs. 107–112.)

Irregular Edges

There are times when even skilled experts produce ragged or irregular cutting. This may be due to faulty glass, a dull cutter, or preoccupation with other matters. Whatever the cause, you can remedy rough edges by one of the following methods:

—If the irregularity is slight, smooth the edge with a hard carborundum stone, of the type used to remove stilt marks from glazed ceramic objects.

—A definite jagged edge requires more than manual strength. If a bench grinder is available, coarse rubber abrasive wheels, electrically driven, are most adequate for actual grinding. For best results, hold the glass at right angles to the wheel. Never attempt grinding with a stone wheel; the inflexibility of such a power-driven wheel is apt to shatter the glass.

Fig. 18. Three candlestands. The bases are cast iron; the trays are glass, drilled after firing for the insertion of the threaded metal spike, which secures the glass tray and holds the candle in place.

—More expensive equipment, including wet belt-driven machines of various sizes and types, can be used.

—Power grinding results in a sanded dull edging which is eradicated by fusing temperatures. Of course, such grinding should only be done before the glass is fired.

DRILLING HOLES

Some projects, such as wind chimes, Christmas ornaments, fountains, and mobiles, require that the glass be pierced. Most glass becomes brittle after firing, and it is usually safer to plan to drill holes immediately after cutting the blank. Be sure to allow for the diameter of the drill used, and don't drill holes too close to the edge of the glass.

Hand Drilling

The simplest and least expensive equipment is a hand drill, commonly called an eggbeater drill, into which a spade (or spear) drill bit is inserted by means of an adjustable chuck.

The glass should be well padded, and since you must use both hands to hold and turn the drill, the glass must be clamped to the table by means of a strong spring-clamp, the inner jaws of which should be cushioned with foam rubber. To center the drill bit, start a small pit mark with the sharp point of a three-cornered file. Then set the drill in vertically and turn the crank handle. When a whitish powdering of the glass appears, add a drop of kerosene to the depression made by the drilling. As the depression widens and deepens, remove the drill and add more kerosene to lubricate and cool both glass and drill bit. Very little pressure is required in this method of drilling, as the weight of the drill is sufficient. When the point of the drill bit is close to the subsurface of the glass, remove the clamp, turn the glass over, and re-clamp it to the table. Start the drilling again directly over the point at which you stopped. Usually one or two turns of the handle will pierce the thin layer of glass, resulting in a clean hole.

The drill bits may be used in an electric hand drill, if the speed of such a drill can be reduced, for a fast drill will shatter the glass. One way of slowing the drill is to use a buffing attachment. Mounted according to the manufacturer's directions for buffing, the attachment is geared to increase the speed of the drill. Many types may be installed in reverse to reduce the speed of the drill, but before purchasing such an attachment, inquire whether it is the reversible type. Procedure in drilling is the same as described for the eggbeater drill.

The Drill Press

The drill press constructed for drilling wood or metal may also be used, by changing the drill bit, for drilling glass. A triangular or prismatic drill bit is stronger for this machine than a spade or spear bit. The speed of the drill press must also be slowed down, and this is generally accomplished by the readjustment of pulley belts or gears provided for the purpose. Most drill press instruction books contain specific information regarding the

speed at which different substances may be drilled. The glass blank need not be clamped to either the floor- or table-type drill press, for this equipment is precision built; the glass can merely be held in place during the drilling. No starting depression is necessary, and the use of the prismatic bit permits drilling without reversing the glass. Drilling is so rapid that kerosene must be applied more frequently than in hand drilling. If holes are to be drilled in the center, or at some point well away from the glass edge, fashion a well of clay to hold enough kerosene to eliminate stopping and starting the drill. Where holes are drilled near the edge, there is usually not enough space for the clay well.

The drilled hole may close during firing of the glass. This can be avoided by packing the hole with a paste made

Fig. 19. A group of glass bowls, drilled through the bottom and mounted on a wrought iron stand.

19

of one of the separators for glass firing moistened with water. After the glass is removed from the kiln, the separator can be ejected with a small tool, and the hole cleaned with a pipe cleaner.

STORING SHEET GLASS

Panels of glass should be kept out of the way, for both your own safety and that of the glass itself. To make a simple yet ingenious rack, place a set of open shelves on its side, thus creating vertical wooden partitions for various types or colors of glass. The rack should be fastened to the wall for strength, and preferably placed on a low platform to make the selection and handling of the glass infinitely easier.

Small sections of glass can be inserted in a wire rack of the type used for phonograph records. Such racks permit instant selection of particular shape or size, and eliminate much of the clutter which results from saving odd bits of glass.

Precut blanks can be stored in boxes or drawers, although too many should not be stacked this way, for layers of glass become quite heavy, and those at the bottom may split from sheer weight.

SAFETY FACTORS

Although glass, especially in broken or irregular segments, is generally considered dangerous, mishaps are always your own fault. The manner in which glass is handled, carelessness on the part of the craftsman, and the condition of the working area are the three common causes of most accidents. All are directly attributable to the glass worker.

Handling the Glass

A sharp glass edge should never be held against the flesh between your thumb and first finger; if there is always a space between the glass and this portion of your hand, there is little chance of getting cut.

Sharp edges are not always distinctly observed. Touching a sharp edge, rather than turning the glass to get a good look at the edge, is never a wise procedure. However, since it seems to be instinctive with the human race to touch things, if you will remember to *roll* your finger along a sharp edge, instead of dragging it with pressure, you will not cut yourself.

Attempting to carry a panel of glass which proves too heavy is a miscalculation which can be hazardous. Ask for help in transporting large sheets of glass, for the weight may cause the panel to slip through your hands.

Strange as it looks in print, many people simply do not watch where they are going. Protruding furniture, storage boxes, raised thresholds—any obstruction can cause a jolt or fall, and if glass is being carried at the time, it will probably shatter. It is therefore especially important that you heed your steps.

Panels of glass should never be replaced carelessly in a storage rack, or indifferently propped against a wall. The slamming of a distant door, the vibration of a heavy truck, or a jet plane overhead, can dislodge a deli-

cately balanced sheet of glass. So remember to store glass carefully.

The Working Area

Litter of any kind is a deterrent to good craftsmanship; glass litter is an invitation to minor or major disaster. Crumbs and tiny shards of glass occur often during glass cutting, and it is imperative that you clear the worktable or cutting board of such particles frequently. In fact, brushing the areas after each blank is cut is an excellent habit to form. A cloth or brush should always be used in cleaning the table; never the bare hands! The floor, too, should be swept at intervals, especially if children or animals are present.

Margins, corners, and odd-shaped segments left over from the cutting of blanks may be saved for jewelry and other small projects. Such scrap glass accumulates rapidly and is usually stored in boxes or bins. Due to the transparency of glass, selection of a particular segment may result in your unintentionally dislodging adjoining shards. The prudent craftsman will use tweezers or tongs to pick up the shards, or at least will wear lightweight garden gloves.

Much of this discussion would seem to indicate that working with glass is extremely difficult. Learning to work with a specific material always presents factors not normally encountered in what is termed everyday living. The characteristics of glass as a material are no more incomprehensible than those connected with crossing the street or baking a cake. They soon become so familiar that correct habits are automatic. Eventually, the glass enthusiast wonders why he was ever hesitant about glass (providing that he even remembers it!).

SUMMARY: THE VARIOUS ASPECTS OF SHEET GLASS

Although sheet glass as an established and definite formation is the main reference point for the techniques of decorating, manipulation, and fusion by heat, which constitute the major portions of this book, how to use blanks and the by-products resulting from cutting the blanks become distinct techniques in their own right, regardless of the decoration you plan or types of glass you use. Therefore, blanks are listed as methods which can apply to any sheet glass:

The Blank

A single thickness of sheet glass; may be fired flat or bent in a mold.

Lamination

Strictly speaking, it is actually the selected materials which are laminated by encasing them within glass.

Fig. 20. The single blank.

Fig. 21. Two blanks for lamination.

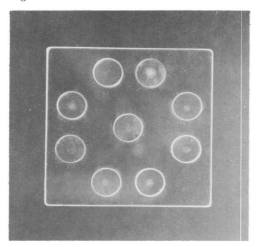

Fig. 22. Partial lamination.

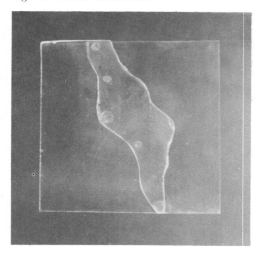

Fig. 23. Partial lamination; overlapping segments.

However, since encasement indicates two or more glass blanks, the term has come to mean the glass itself, in ordinary parlance.

Partial Lamination

Segments are placed on the blank as decorative or functional additions. Differentiated from full lamination by not being of dimensions equal to the blank.

Fragmentation

The overlapping of glass sections, usually in irregular shard form.

Crushings

The finest particles to be procured from the original glass, and still identifiable as such.

FIRING

The verb "fire" has been defined as (a) to retain fire, as to "fire" a furnace; (b) to temper with heat, as to "fire" pottery. The two meanings can be confusing to one who is unfamiliar with ceramic terminology, for the first specifically refers to equipment; the second, to the material which is being heat-treated, with the implication that any device transmitting heat can be used. The word fire, in the ceramic craft field, is generally understood to indicate the use of closed ovens, with the proper insulation to withstand heat specified by the manufacturer, as opposed to furnaces, which, in other areas, can designate open flame or blowers for the express purpose of melting ores or metallic compounds. While torches might be used to heat such clay or ceramic bodies as would

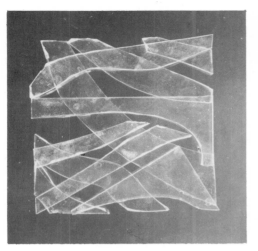

Fig. 24. Fragmentation; irregular shards.

Fig. 25. Crushings.

resist sudden and intense fire, I doubt that glaze-firing by this means could be done satisfactorily. Certainly the thermal shock of applying a high degree of temperature to glass is for laboratory experimentation, and not for the craftsman whose main goal is to translate his preconceived design into tangible form. In the following section, therefore, please understand that all reference to firing pertains to the closed kiln as the selected equipment.

In addition, since this book is devoted, with few exceptions, to techniques dealing with sheet glass, firing can be construed to be of sufficient temperature to change the original form of the glass, rather than to merely set or bake colorants at low temperatures which would leave the glass formation unchanged.

The Cycle of Glass Subjected to Heat

It is a predominant characteristic of glass that it must always move when subjected to heat. If you know what is occurring, even in a closed kiln, you will be able to terminate the application of heat at any given temperature in order to control the glass, and thus produce a planned project. There are definite stages of movement between which changes in structure are plainly discernible:

1—Up to 1000°F.: Sheet glass remains a rigid blank, although it is expanding invisibly.

2—From 1000 to 1250°F.: No apparent change.

3—From 1250 to 1300°F.: The edges of extremely thin glass start to "blunt"; in the bending process, the glass begins to ease itself into the mold cavity or depression. In single-strength glass, there is no change.

4—From 1300 to 1350°F.: Edges of stained glass start to blunt; bent pieces begin to sag. There is no apparent change in single- or double-strength colorless commercial glass.

5—From 1350 to 1400°F.: Edges of stained glass are fully rounded; bent pieces are almost completely

Fig. 26. Fragmentation.

sagged. Jewels have begun to contract, starting the balling process. (There is exactly the same amount of glass as there was before firing; when the glass contracts, it must go somewhere, and a vertical thickening takes place.) Commercial glass, being harder, starts blunting edges, and sags slightly, if bent.

6—From 1400 to 1450°F.: Stained glass jewels become fully rounded and cabochon in shape. Commercial glass may be completely bent, or very nearly so, depending on its hardness, and the type of kiln used.

7—From 1450 to 1500°F.: Distortion of stained glass begins; tiny needlepoints take form, and the structure flattens somewhat. The underside, or subsurface, lifts, probably due to air trapped beneath. Commercial glass, again depending on the glass and/or the kiln, may either be ideally sagged, or beginning to "needlepoint."

8—Beyond 1500°F.: Further distortion takes place. Stained glass continues lifting, beginning to form a bubble, or bubbles. Commercial glass forms extreme needlepoints, and any surface colorants begin to recede from the outer edge inward.

24

It is during the lifting of either type of glass that a "fold-over" can occur; i.e., still inclined toward sheet form, although distorted, the glass may suddenly collapse, folding over such areas as are continuing to sag. Usually a new bubble starts, if heating is prolonged. Unless heat is terminated, the bubble, or bubbles, will burst, and the resulting opening will heal. From then on, overfiring of the glass will result in a molten mass which, when cooled, may or may not fracture.

This is the cycle of fired glass. Somewhere within this cycle lies the correct terminal point of temperature for successful firing.

Separators

Glass, during its firing cycle, becomes soft, then viscous, and finally molten. During any of these stages, there will be a complete or partial adherence to the kiln shelf, mold, or other furniture on which it is being fired. Unless you intend to bond glass to another material, the supporting

Fig. 27. A glass Christmas wreath—fragmentation. (Work of Jean Ulm.)

Fig. 28. Fragmentation of stained glass. Two suspensions—figure forms.

structure should be separated from the glass to ensure removal after firing.

For most types of colorless commercial sheet glass, ceramic grade whiting (also known as calcium carbonate) has proved satisfactory, and may be applied to the shelf or mold in several ways:

Spraying

Mix the whiting with water to a consistency which will pass through the orifice of the specific spray equipment you are using. Sprayers can be of the compressor type, or the popular small vacuum variety. Unless there is a wide adjustment range, air brushes are too fine to permit adequate coverage.

Brushing

Mix the whiting with water and apply with a brush. Porous surfaces, such as clay or firebrick, absorb the water content quickly, and should be dampened first. The pressure of the brush is apt to leave high ridges, edges, or textured surfaces bare, and a second light coat of whiting should be applied to these. Overlapping brush strokes result in ridges to a certain degree, and this ridging can often serve as a deliberate texture pattern.

Dry Sifting

Sift the whiting through a fine tea strainer or sieve. All bare areas must be adequately covered. Although the whiting is as finely milled as flour, the weight of the glass will not flatten it out, but will form over any uneven bumps or excess sifting, thus distorting the true shape. If the basket of the strainer is never more than half full, it is easier to control the sifting of the whiting. Should the coat of whiting appear to be bumpy, quickly brush it back into the container, and re-sift.

Whether sprayed, painted, or sifted, the whiting must be thoroughly dry before firing. Like the chemicals of overglaze and metallic overglaze, moist whiting creates fumes which must be driven from the kiln. When lowering the glass blank into position, do not move or shift the whiting in the process. Whiting must be discarded after each firing, for it changes chemically to an oxide, which will most probably stick to another piece of glass in subsequent firings.

In stacking the kiln, be sure to provide ample air circulation, not only to prevent deflection of the fumes back onto the glass, but to assure even sagging. A minimum of two inches between the top of the glass and the shelf above it is required; three to four inch spacing is better.

Other Separators

Although whiting is most universally used as a separator, there are other types which meet specific needs. These include plaster of Paris, dry clay, graphite, alumina hydrate, aluminum foil, sheet mica, refractory materials used for high temperature welding in the aircraft industry; and finally a formula from my own laboratories, consisting of three special ingredients, each of which offsets any disadvantages inherent in the other two. Simply designated as "moldcoat," this mixture is as nearly foolproof as two years of experimentation can produce. To date, we have found no type of glass which attracts or is disfigured by this separator. Re-usable, it can be brushed or sprayed on clay and metal molds or shelves.

Of the listed separators, the following are useful for flat firing only, on kiln shelves, fire brick, or clay tiles:

Sheet mica, which must be peeled from the main section in extremely thin layers, or it will swell, causing the glass to lift.

Aircraft refractories.

Aluminum foil, which can leave a metallic residue on the glass.

The other separators may be sifted on either shelving or concave molds. Dry clay, plaster of Paris, alumina hydrate, and graphite deposit a film or discoloration on the subsurface of varying types of glass, although not uniformly on all.

Kilns

Definite firing predictions are difficult to make for any particular type of kiln. Generally speaking, enameling kilns give good results, although but one piece can be fired at a time. Unlike copper enameling, glass cannot be removed from the kiln while hot, or even warm. While the glass never becomes fluid at bending temperature, it expands considerably, and during the cooling process it must contract. Even when the pyrometer on a kiln indicates room temperature, if the shelves or mold are slightly warmer, the sagged piece may crack suddenly, or subsequently upon removal from the kiln. Considering that finished glassware can be washed in hot water, this may seem confusing. Actually, while cooling it is going through an evolution as definite as the sagging, which may be observed visually. This phase is termed annealing, and is the adjusting and hardening of the glass into its new and permanent form. Commercial factories use annealing ovens called "lehrs," which are set at low temperatures to maintain an even heat during the annealing. With simple studio equipment, and without the need to keep a constant production level, the craftsman finds it quite satisfactory merely to allow the kiln to cool naturally and completely.

The Enamel Kiln

Enameling kilns are constructed to produce the greatest heat in the least time. Glass requires a cool start, with a slow and gradual rise in temperature. To allow for this seeming inconsistency, the door is left slightly ajar during the first part of the firing. If the kiln is equipped with a pyrometer, it should read 1000°F. before the door

is closed. Depending on the size of the kiln, this takes from one hour for an 8x9" kiln, to an hour and a half for a larger kiln. The kiln should be checked frequently after the door is closed, since some kilns attain high temperature rapidly and, again, a pyrometer is most useful. A small kiln, wired only around the sides, attains complete sagging temperature and rounded edges at 1500°F. Without the aid of a pyrometer, sagging will have to be checked visually, by the appearance of the bending contour; the area of glass nearest the back coils will be bright orange in color. Kilns of this type are always cooler directly in front of the door, and unless the shape is very small, the front edges of the glass will be more angular than those at the back.

The kiln shelf or mold may be removed from the kiln long enough to turn it around and replace it, to give the cooler edges a little more heat. Needless to say, the hot shelf or mold must be placed on a fireproof surface, and you should work rapidly and with the utmost caution. An enameling fork or spatula is not strong enough to remove the heavy equipment and glass, but a satisfactory tool can be improvised by flattening a shovel of the size used to fill coal scuttles. Most of the larger enameling kilns are wired on the floor as well as the sides, which ensures a more uniform heat with no cool areas. This type of kiln attains full sagging at 1450°F., and no turning of the glass is required.

One type of enameling kiln features the element installed in the top of the kiln. This direct heat, most desirable for enameling, tends to start the lique-faction of the sheet glass before the blank can sag gradually into the mold cavity. Sudden application of heat, as well as sudden cooling, creates thermal shock that results in fracturing or bubbling of the glass. At the present time there seems to be no solution to this problem, as glass demands an atmospheric temperature rise, rather than direct heat.

The Ceramic Kiln

Ceramic kilns, with the exception of the small test kilns, gain temperature slowly, and no special precautions need be taken for the safety of the glass. However, there are usually colorants, lusters, or adhesives to affix loose material to the base glass and all of these produce fumes which must be allowed to escape. Failure to provide for this results in a frosty or clouded appearance on the glass, and in the case of overglaze and metallic overglazes, discoloration and scum may appear. If the kiln is well vented by propping open the lid (or the door, in a front-loading kiln) ½″ until 1000°F. is reached, these disfigurements may be avoided. Kilns lacking pyrometric equipment will be approximately 1000°F. when an 022 cone bends half over. The average ceramic kiln should reach sagging temperature between 1450° and 1500°F.

The Porcelain Kiln

The so-called high-fire kiln has heavier wiring and insulation, designed to safely attain higher temperatures than the ceramic kiln. The procedure for firing is identical to that for the ceramic kiln; however, because of the construction and greater retention of heat, the high-fire kiln softens and bends glass at approximately 1450°F., or an 016 cone.

The Gas Kiln

Gas-fired kilns have two characteristics generally lacking in the electric kilns. The first is slower cooling, providing a "soaking" atmosphere which matures clay bodies and glazes, but which can prove disastrous in firing glass. There is a wide firing range for ceramic bodies and glazes, during which a slight underfiring or overfiring is not discernible. This leeway of flexibility is not present in glass firing, and mere seconds determine failure or success. To prevent overfiring, even though the kiln has been shut off, the lid or door may be propped open a half inch for 15 minutes. (The electric kiln, although it cools rapidly and does not have a soaking atmosphere, can also overfire glass unless it is vented in the same manner, allowing 3 to 30 minutes, depending on the size of the kiln.)

The second characteristic of gas kilns is that of the fuel itself. Many areas supply natural gas, which contains varying quantities of sulphur. Glass and many glass colorants, including lusters and gold, are extremely sensitive to the presence of sulphur in the kiln. Discoloration and frosted surfaces can be attributed to atmospheric contamination by impurities in the fuel, as well as by trapped fumes or condensation. The obvious remedy is to vent kilns in the initial stages; also to vent them for a short period immediately after the heat has been shut off.

As is the case with possible materials of which I am unaware, there may be a brand of kiln, or custom-built kiln, which does not perform according to the statements in the preceding section. If there is a kiln which cools too fast for natural annealing, heat may be retained in the firing chamber by packing all doors or other openings, including peepholes, with asbestos packing or asbestos rope, immediately after firing ceases. In the case of experimental firing of exceedingly thick or slab glass, a rheostat may be connected to the kiln to maintain specified temperatures between definite temperature declines. Such equipment calls for technical ceramic engineering knowledge, and it would be wise to consult firms who maintain a competent staff for this purpose.

Summary

It seems obvious that the firing of the glass blank, however embellished, determines success or failure. Regardless of the craftsmanship or artistry employed, if the firing or cooling cycle is hurried, disaster follows. This is one phase of the entire procedure where judgment can be erroneous, and guesswork is to be shunned like the plague. There are basic principles pertaining to the refractory nature of glass substances; an understanding of, and co-operation with, these principles assure success.

Venting the kiln does not, as is often the case in ceramic firing, consist of merely removing peephole plugs. Removal of the plugs may assist in cooling the kiln, but will not permit the complete escape of fumes, or condensation of moisture. Venting, as applied to glass bending, means propping of the lid or door to a half-inch opening.

There is no prescribed formula applicable to specific firing temperatures. Two kilns, identical as to size, model number, and brand, do not necessarily fire at the same rate. It can almost be assumed that kilns, like humans, have individual personalities. There are two extremes of firing which are perceivable, and by the observation of which the specific kiln can be scheduled to give good results. The under-fired glass will retain angular, although not sharp, edges. This appearance in itself is not objectionable; however, it is usually an indication that the blank has not sagged completely into the mold cavity, and the resultant bent piece may "rock." Over-firing, on the other hand, creates innumerable tiny needlepoints of glass around the edges of the fired shape, and any colorant on the surface recedes from the outer edge. Between these two extremes lies the correct temperature for any specified kiln. By using an 014 cone bent half over, or a pyrometer reading of 1500°F. as a basis for comparison on the first firing, the craftsman can determine how his kiln is reacting. If the test piece indicates underfiring, the pyrometer can read 1550°F. or the 014 cone allowed to touch the shelf, on the next firing. If the test firing produces symptoms of overfiring, the temperature can be cut to a 1450°F. reading, or an 016 cone fired flat.

Kiln conditions can account for varied temperatures: prolonged use may have slightly warped the insulating brick, resulting in some leakage and cool spots, although the position of the cone or pyrometer is in a hotter atmosphere; salt air or age may have corroded the elements in an electric kiln, thus slowing down one portion of the kiln. (Elements can be cleaned by firing an empty kiln with a small handful of moth balls in the firing chamber. The corrosion will be deposited in the kiln in the form of black flakes, and this, of course, is the reason for not firing glass at the same time.)

The distance from the electrical source has a definite bearing on the temperature gain. Loss of power may occur when the kiln is situated at a remote point, particularly if extension cords—even heavy-duty type—are used.

The type or brand of glass is also an important factor in determining the firing temperature. Hard, brittle glass usually requires more heat. Needless to say, a variety of soft and hard glass, fired at the same time, must prove disappointing in one way or another. A good rule is to use the same type of sheet glass, if not the same brand, in any one firing.

Flat panels, jewelry, etc., which are fired on a kiln shelf or firebrick, are uniformly exposed to the atmosphere of the kiln, and require approximately 50°F. less heat than for the bending temperature of any specified glass.

Spacing the intervals of turning on lower and upper elements is a controversial subject. Only by experimenting can you determine whether a glass kiln should be fired in sequence, or all switches turned on simultaneously, holding back the too-rapid rise in temperature by venting the kiln.

MOLDS FOR BENDING

Introductory

To compel the flat glass blank to assume a three-dimensional shape, place it over a hollow or concave depression in the structure on which it is fired. Such a structure is called a mold. Unlike ceramic molds, which are generally made of plaster of Paris for the express purpose of reproducing the desired model in clay, the glass mold must accompany the blank through the firing cycle. It must therefore withstand heat without collapse or warping. Metal molds are generally used in commercial glass bending for light fixtures; these are expensive because dies must be made for each size and shape, and unless you are also a blacksmith, or skilled in metal and welding processes, it is virtually impossible for you to essay metal mold construction.

The clay mold, like all clay projects, presents the greatest latitude for creative flexibility with minimum required skill. There are certain factors, to be sure, that determine proportion, strength, and suitability of the mold, but these are not difficult to comprehend. The ultimate satisfaction of producing an entirely original glass form more than compensates for the effort of making, drying, and firing the mold.

The Terra-Cotta Mold

The terra-cotta mold is, at one and the same time, a fired pottery object, and a form upon which glass blanks may be fired innumerable times.

The mold cavity provides the exact shape of the outside of the glass form, and must be fashioned with care. There can be no undercuts, and the bottom of the mold cavity must be absolutely level, or the resulting glass piece will "rock."

Terra cotta, a heavily grogged clay, is used for the molds; since the mold may be fired many times, the fine particles of fired clay help to provide a somewhat porous body that will withstand the shock of alternate heating and cooling, occurring each time sheet glass is bent upon the mold. The clay may be any color, but red is desirable, since a dark color is best for determining the thickness of the separator used to prevent the glass from sticking to the clay mold.

There are several ways of making the mold. Perhaps the easiest is to drape a sheet of clay over an inverted bowl or plate. If you want an irregular shape, cut or carve the model for the cavity from plaster of a proper thickness to give the desired depth. Avoid steep vertical sides; the inverted model should slope gradually from its widest point at the base, to a narrower diameter at the top level. Cover the model with tissue paper and cellophane-tape it to the underside of the model. Apply a damp sponge with a firm, gentle pressure, working from the top to the bottom edge of the model, thus smoothing the folds and creases which inevitably occur in covering three-dimensional shapes. Then place the model upon the plaster bat, still inverted, with the widest diameter contacting the bat.

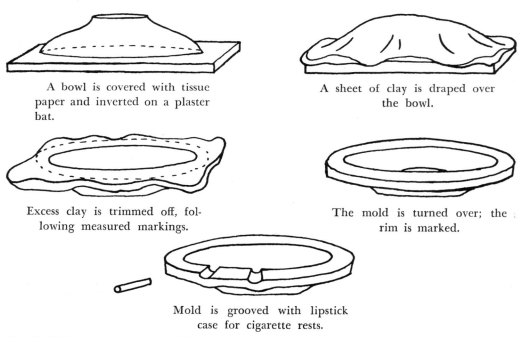

A bowl is covered with tissue paper and inverted on a plaster bat.

A sheet of clay is draped over the bowl.

Excess clay is trimmed off, following measured markings.

The mold is turned over; the rim is marked.

Mold is grooved with lipstick case for cigarette rests.

Fig. 29. Making a terra-cotta mold.

Next, roll a thick coil of terra cotta and lay it around the model where it joins the bat. It is advisable to hold the model in place with one hand while placing the coil in position with the other, to prevent shifting. Flatten the coil against the model and the plaster bat, thus filling in the acute angle between the two. Score this section of clay with a wooden tool to ensure a perfect joining with the sheet of clay which is to be draped over the model. If the coil is moist, additional bonding is unnecessary; if of stiff consistency, water or slip may be added to the scored marks as a binder.

Any slightly absorbent surface, such as smooth unfinished wood, plaster, canvas, or the underside of oilcloth, may be used to roll out the sheet of clay. Marble, glass, or enameled surfaces are undesirable, as the moist clay will not come away from a nonporous surface. Place two wooden sticks, three-fourths or one inch thick (depending on the size of the mold) parallel upon the working surface, and roll the clay on top of them with a rolling pin. The wooden sticks maintain a uniform thickness, and the size of the sheet of clay is controlled by the amount used. Smoothness can be obtained by turning the mass often until it has been entirely leveled between the sticks.

Center the sheet of smooth clay carefully on the inverted model, and allow it to drape over the sides. Enough clay should have been used in the rolling process to provide an extension of several inches onto the bat. Pass the rolling pin lightly over the top to find the exact center of the mold, but never with great enough pressure to stretch the sheet of clay, since this will weaken the mold. The original thickness must be maintained, for a weakened mold often splits under the weight of the glass during the firing. To prevent stretching, roll a piece of wooden doweling, 6″ long and about 1″ thick, from the outside toward the center, and up the slope of the hump made by the model. If you hold your left hand firmly on the top as you roll the dowel toward it, the sheet of clay will not move or wrinkle against the model. Apply firm pressure at the angle where the model rests on the bat, thus creating the definite shape for the cavity of the mold.

The insert model must be left in the draped clay shell until the clay has stiffened enough to support its own weight without warping. However, since the stiffening is accomplished by the evaporation of moisture, shrinking is inevitable, sometimes causing fine cracks or fissures to appear. If you remove the insert model before the clay shell dries, you can smooth these fissures and surface cracks with fingertips or wooden clay tools. When the clay can be handled without distortion, turn the mold over and trim off the outside edges. These edges may correspond exactly to the shape of the insert piece, or they may be cut on a free-form line as desired. When a satisfactory shape has been selected and trimmed, carefully loosen the edges of tissue paper and cellophane tape, and remove the model. The tissue can then be peeled from the mold without damage. Infrared heat lamps may be used to speed the drying process. Suspend them about 14″ above the mold; the heat penetrates the clay and cuts the drying time about in half.

Execute incised lines, patterns, or texturing before the mold dries. High relief design or intaglio patterns must not be undercut, and texture can be supplied by means of coarse combs, forks, or ceramic tools. Light texturing will not show as a final glass indentation, and any design should be simple and well defined. If design is accomplished by adding small flat pieces of clay, coat such additions with slip, and weld them to the mold with a wooden tool.

Lipstick cases of various sizes are fine for grooving cigarette rests, or fluting edges around an entire mold. Since the sheet glass to be sagged is ⅛″ to 3⁄16″ thick (the thickness being determined by the size of the mold), be sure to make allowance for this in cutting cigarette rests, so that the finished glass ashtray has sufficient room for the cigarette to be cradled without rolling off. It is a wise precaution to roll a thick slab of clay, six inches square, grooving several widths and depths with assorted tubes. Test pieces of glass, sagged on this tile, will be a guide in determining the proper grooving for the selected thickness of glass.

Any texturing on the bottom of the cavity must be kept perfectly level, or the glass will not rest evenly upon a table; some glass workers leave the bottom of the cavity untextured. A flange, or rim, is always provided around the edge of the cavity to support the sheet of glass until the sagging starts; otherwise it may slip into the mold. As the glass sags, air is displaced in the mold cavity. If the rim surrounding the cavity is perfectly flat, the trapped air will blow a bubble over the cavity. To avoid this, drill several holes, about 1⁄16″ in diameter, through the sides of the mold at approximately half the depth. Openings of this size allow the air to escape without being apparent on the surface of the bent glass.

The mold should be dried slowly, upside down on a level plaster bat, with a light weight on top; corners are also weighted if the mold is square or triangular in shape. When dry, sand the outside bottom of the mold level, so that the glass will sag evenly in the mold. To keep the rim even during its final firing shrinkage, fire the mold upside down. Molds will last longer if they are fired two to four cones lighter than the recommended maturing temperature for the particular clay used. Glass is never fired as high as a matured clay body, and underfiring seems to secure greater elasticity for the constant shock of repeated glass firings.

Molds may be thrown on a wheel to obtain round shapes, and should, of course, be as thick as in the draping procedure. The size of the finished piece should always be considered, and rims should never be so wide, in proportion to the cavity, that the glass piece is topheavy. In planning the finished size, always consider the shrinkage of the mold. If the glass piece demands exact measurements, make the mold larger to allow for shrinkage.

Precautionary Notes

The use of two or more different types of clay in constructing a terra-cotta mold can result in conflicting shrinkages, which may cause separation of the various strata, cracking, or warping. Always use clay from the same batch.

Uneven rolling of the clay, or stretching over the model, weakens the mold. Severance of the mold at weak points often occurs when the glass blank is being fired.

The rigid model for the mold cavity cannot be compressed by the shrinkage of the drying clay. Always remove the model before shrinkage is great enough to cause an open split.

Gouges or nicks in the bottom of the mold create protuberances on the ultimate glass piece, causing it to be uneven. Keep the bottom smooth and level.

The mold should not be noticeably higher at one point than another, for the glass blank fired in a slanting position is apt to shift off center in loading and firing the kiln.

Failure to provide for the escape of expanding air within the mold cavity during the firing causes the glass blank to form a balloon-like bubble. Provide vents or holes if the model does not incorporate channels in the original design.

Forced drying often warps the mold. Dry the mold slowly at room temperature until the clay starts turning light in color.

Summary

As a rule, cast ceramic bisque shapes cannot safely be used as molds. Clay bodies which are fired to maturity do not withstand the shock of repeated heating and cooling. Depending on the shape of the interior and the relationship of the depth to the uppermost dimensions, a cast ceramic shape seldom provides strength and durability as a mold. The splitting of a cast ceramic mold during the firing causes considerable damage to the kiln, as the glass blank is apt to shatter into countless bits which fuse to kiln shelves and heating elements. Remember that the terra-cotta mold is an instrument for producing glass shapes, and not an exhibition piece. Over-adornment and intricate modeling, although well defined on the clay, are distorted and vague when viewed through the thickness of the finished glass shape.

Clay molds, even though properly dried and fired, often have a tendency to split or crack during the first glass firing, if the mold is placed too close to the elements of an electric kiln, if the shelf above is too close to the mold, or if the kiln is cooled too rapidly. Since cracking of the mold does not seem to occur on subsequent firings under these conditions, it would seem that a curing process takes place during the first glass firing. Refiring the mold without the glass does not eliminate the possibility of cracking; the mold seems to "cure" only when the glass blank is fired upon it. Always allow ample air circulation during the first glass firing, placing the mold and glass blank well away from the kiln elements, and cooling the kiln slowly.

Molds which have been split, either

from being placed too near the kiln elements, from being cooled too rapidly, or from falling to the floor, may be mended by coating the thickness of the clay shell on the two adjoining sections, with silicate of soda (water glass). After drying, seal the pores of the clay by adding another coating to one section, and bind both pieces together with wire or tape. Excess silicate of soda must be removed from the surface and the bottom of the mold before drying, for silicate of soda is an elementary form of glass, and will become viscous when fired. Forty-eight hours' drying time should be allowed before firing.

Other Types of Molds

Two other methods of producing supported hollows or cavities for sagged glass, are worth mentioning. Both types are composed of materials which crumble easily, and consequently have a relatively short life span. And neither is suitable for delicate or precise detail. These limitations, however, are decidedly offset by various advantages: they need not be prefired, there is no shrinkage, and they are simple to execute, even for children.

Firebrick Molds

Soft firebrick can be hollowed quite simply, using kitchen spoons and knives as carving tools. It is very difficult to achieve an absolutely flat surface in the bottom of the cavity by such means because of the coarse nature of the material and the awkwardness of handling tools within the cavity. If the lowest level is irregular,

the glass sagged on it will be correspondingly irregular, resulting in a glass shape which rocks.

Solution of the problem lies in planning a two-piece mold. The brick is severed horizontally lengthwise with a hacksaw blade. Set aside the lower half; this will become the flat, even bottom of the mold.

Place the upper section, with the cut side up, on the workbench. Since these bricks are manufactured by vacuum or pressure processes, the outer surfaces are usually finer grained and somewhat harder than the more porous centers, and are therefore used for the area where exact joining is essential.

As described in the section on terracotta molds, the sides of the mold cavity should be gently sloping rather than vertical, for the successful sagging of the glass blank. The desired angle and the measurements of both upper and lower levels should be sketched on paper. The upper dimensions should not extend to the outer edges of the brick; leaving a rim of at least ½" provides a secure resting place for the glass blank, as well as strengthening to some extent the edges of the brick.

Mark the shape and size of the lower dimensions on the smooth side of the half-brick (that portion which was the outer facing of the brick), and cut with a sharp, slender knife straight through the brick thickness. If the knife blade is not long enough to penetrate the upper surface, a slanting cut can be established from the *inside* of the portion to be removed, to the outer or true measurement, thus removing a wedge of firebrick. Then reinsert the knife, and complete the cutting.

Turn over the half-section of brick and sketch the upper outline. It is simple, then, to cut the desired cavity on the predetermined angle, whether the cavity is to be angular, and accomplished with a straight knife, or curved, requiring the use of a spoon, peach pitter, or other scooping tool.

The two sections, of course, would be apt to shift if not secured together. They should be taped firmly, and porcelain or metal rods pushed through both half-bricks. This is a permanent positioning, and the rods should not be removed. The tape can be removed after the rods are inserted.

The unit is given a complete coating of kiln wash, including the underside of the mold, as kiln wash helps to seal the porous surfaces, and to strengthen the somewhat fragile structure. After drying, it can then be given any of the treatments suggested as separators for glass.

Asbestos Molds

Powdered asbestos, used by plumbers to insulate pipes against freezing conditions, and to retain as much heat as possible in hot-water piping, can be mixed with hot water—a little at a time—until it is of doughlike consistency, then kneaded into a homogenized mass and applied over an inverted form covered with tissue paper, as outlined for the terra-cotta mold. The main difference between the two materials is that terra cotta can be rolled into a uniformly thick sheet, whereas the asbestos cannot, but must be applied to the form by the handful. Join the applications by gentle patting. As this material lacks the strength of clay, the minimum thickness should be one inch. The asbestos shell should not be disturbed until it is entirely dry, because of the fragility of the structure.

When dry, the outside can be sprayed with lacquer, which will fire out, but meanwhile will provide some strength for removal from the rigid model. After carefully removing the asbestos shell, check it for any gaps where applications have failed to fill in joinings; pack any such gaps with the wet asbestos mix, firmly pressing the tissue paper against the outer shell. If the tissue is loose, it should be removed, but the utmost care should be taken not to separate or tear the outer walls of the shell. High spots can be carefully scraped off.

After the first glass firing, the shell will be hardened to a certain extent, although it will never have the strength of a clay mold. If the craftsman is expert at hand modeling, this material is excellent for shaping a mold without a model. It is especially good for fashioning small removable "bridges," which may be positioned as desired to force the necks of long bottles to form a handle or otherwise sag into an interesting shape. (See Chapter on Bottle Bending.) Both interior and exterior of the mold should be brushed or sprayed with kiln wash, after which the mold is ready for the application of one of the glass separators.

Cast-Iron Molds

Any of the preformed cast-iron trays or bowls can be used as molds, with certain precautions in mind. Iron will rust if moisture is applied and there is a delay before firing. Apply liquid separators, therefore, just before the glass firing, drying such applications very rapidly by forced heat, such as hot air dryers. If dried in an oven, permit steam to escape by leaving the oven door ajar. Some cast-iron forms have been found to flash a rust oxidation onto the glass blank despite rapid drying of the separator. A certain amount of disintegration of the iron form takes place with repeated firings, causing the form to become pitted.

CUTTING PATTERNS TO FIT THE MOLD

Mold is turned over on paper and an outline drawn.

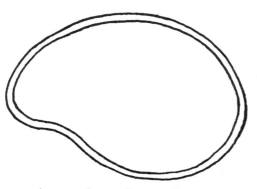

A second, smaller outline is drawn within the original.

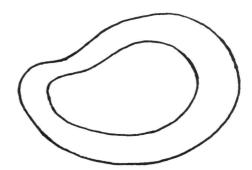

The smaller outline is cut, paper turned over, and cavity indicated.

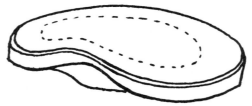

The cut glass shape is placed on the mold.

Fig. 30. Cutting patterns to fit the mold.

FREE-FORM GLASS BLANKS ON BASIC MOLDS

It is quite possible to evolve a wide variety of bent forms from one basic mold, simply by changing the patterns for the glass blanks. The mold cavity should have a rather small bottom diameter and gently sloping sides, without irregular indentations. It should be uniform in measurements, the length equaling the width. Round molds are generally more satisfactory for this procedure than square or triangular molds, since the corner angles are apt to distort circle or free-form blanks. On the other hand, square or triangular blanks bend quite naturally on round molds, while retaining the original contour or outline. In planning a pattern, the only stipulation is that the blank should extend a minimum of ¾″ beyond the line of demarcation formed by the flat bottom and the sloping sides; otherwise, the bent shape will be flat on the bottom (as the mold is flat) but will not retain liquids, food, or ashes. The blank should not extend beyond the edges of the mold. The blank, of course, can be decorated as desired. Full coverage colorants, overglazes, liquid overglazes, and gold etched with liquid glass are excellent media for surface decoration.

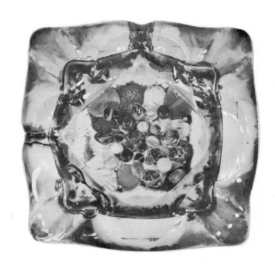

C. LAMINATION

PRELUDE TO LAMINATION

Webster's New World Dictionary defines the verb "laminate" as follows: "to form . . . into a thin sheet. To cover with thin layers. To make by building up in layers." "Laminated" (adjective): "composed of or arranged into thin sheets or layers."

This general term, of course, can apply to any material, such as wood, plastic, metal, or cloth. For the specific category of fused glass, references will pertain only to such materials as lie within the limitations (or scope) of glass.

When and What to Laminate. Just as there must be a reason for any thought or action, so must there be a justification for lamination. It is not reasonable to assume that certain colorants or materials should be laminated, if the tendencies of the materials are in conflict with those of the sheet glass encasing them, or if their best qualities would result from some other treatment. The following may be used for lamination:

Essential Materials

Copper Enamels

When used as a colorant, ground or lump enamels present a problem of adherence to the exposed surface of sheet glass. Since enamels expand dur-

Fig. 31. Three-layer lamination. (*Lower blank*) All-over sifting of ceramic frit and calcined gold mica flakes. (*Center blank*) Black ceramic underglaze outline of bird design. (*Upper blank*) Pink and purple overglaze color patches within outlines of birds; metallic overglaze border lines.

ing the firing, and contract when cooling, at a different rate than that of the glass, they have a tendency to loosen in patches. By laminating the enamels, they cannot separate from the glass, and are sealed between the two sheets.

Underglaze

Ceramic underglazes provide an excellent medium for design. However, they lack ingredients which produce a glossy, protective surface; they may be softened to the point of disintegration when the glass object is washed, and being absorbent, are easily soiled. Lamination provides the necessary shield for these pigments.

Metals

Most metals release from the glass after firing. Sterling, copper, brass, iron, or nichrome wire may be laminated, thus preventing the release. Wire is utilized as a linear design ele-

42

ment, and all but the sterling silver oxidizes, turning black. The lamination of sheet metal of any kind is a matter of judgment. Too thick or too large sections may fracture one or both sheets of glass. Aluminum, copper, or brass screen may be successfully laminated. Aluminum screen may retain its original appearance, darken, or produce opalescent tints, depending on the processing and brand. The use

of metals should be restricted to flat panels, for the glass sheets, when bent, become flexible, while the metals remain rigid, and these two conflicting reactions usually fracture the glass.

Fiberglass

Fiberglass threads and screen, because of finer composition, tend to disappear when exposed to direct heat on glass surfaces. Protected by the

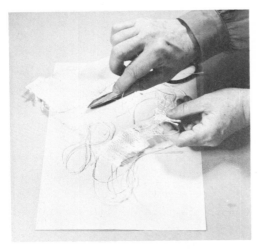
Fig. 32. Threads are unraveled from yardage.

Fig. 33. Individual threads are brushed with ceramic underglaze.

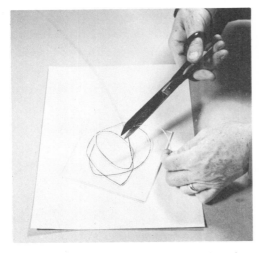
Fig. 34. The thread is coiled on the glass blank; the uncoated end is severed.

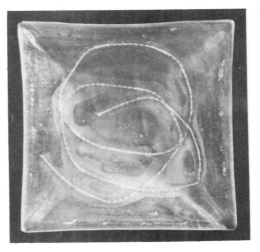
Fig. 35. The fired piece.

upper glass blank, they retain their composition. They may be colored with underglaze or overglaze.

Mica

Mica is introduced in flake form, to produce bubbles or texture. These flakes puff during the firing and raise the glass directly over them. Control of the bubbles lies in the size and thickness of the individual flakes. Applied to exposed glass surfaces, they cannot fulfill their function, and result in rough, dull particles.

Optional Materials

Overglaze

Some overglaze colors are dulled, or assume an entirely different hue when laminated. As most overglazes are prepared with some sort of oil, they emit fumes which must be burned out in a light prefiring before lamination. Since this is time-consuming, and since overglazes are actually more brilliant when fired on the top surface, it seems expedient to omit laminating them except in those treatments where the effect of depth is desired.

Glass Glaze

Coatings of glass glaze become fluid after the two glass blanks have started to fuse together. The glass glaze "boils" just before smoothing out. Since the glass blanks cannot permit the resulting expanded air to escape, unplanned bubbles and granules form, which are undesirable in a bent piece, but may be effective for underseas panels.

Lusters

Glass lusters which are brilliant on surfaces, provide only coloring when laminated. Like overglazes, they must be prefired before laminating.

Stained Glass

Bits of stained glass become viscous before window, texture, or plate glass. Much of their three-dimensional quality is lost in lamination. When allowed to fuse to glass surfaces, each type can fire individually; when laminated, the different expansions can create stress in the glass blanks, often causing fractures in the fused unit. Finely crushed stained glass, however, becomes a layer of color or colors, bonding the sheet glass together. Discretion must be used in selecting the fineness of grind.

Enamel Threads

Processing of enamel threads shrinks this form of enamel for copper. The threads can either be laminated or fused to the upper surface of the glass.

Silver and Gold Foils for Enameling

These are effective either on upper surfaces, or laminated. Both tend to be slightly more metallic in lamination.

It is apparent that glass and any materials to be laminated must have a relationship which will permit perfect fusing without discoloration or fracturing of the finished piece. Disappointment and discouragement are best eliminated by test-firing dubious or unknown types of colorants. Plastics, cloth, sequins, cereals, and other such combustible matter burn away, usually leaving an ash residue. A knowledge of the characteristics of ceramic or mineral constituents is essential for successful lamination, whether such knowledge be gained from precedent or from personal experience.

TEXTURE

For most of us, the fascination of glass lies in the sparkle and clarity of the material. The illusion of greater depth can be achieved by entrapping air between two blanks. This simple form of lamination can be effected by the introduction of uncalcined mica flakes which swell during the firing, usually after the edges of the two blanks have fused together. Sealed edges and minute glass areas between flakes result in considerable pressure of air expanding from the mica, actually causing the upper blank to rise above each flake, thus creating countless bubbles.

Practical procedure consists of first oiling the lower blank, for dry materials need some sort of bonding to hold them in place on the smooth glass. A band of some light oil which is not highly volatile, is brushed around the perimeter of the blank. ("Baby oil," i.e., cosmetic oil for infants, is excellent for this purpose.) Distribute the oil with the palm of the hand over the entire surface, for even this light oil creates fumes when heavily applied. The use of cloth or paper to distribute the oil would remove all traces, whereas hand distribution leaves a residual film on the glass.

Sift the mica flakes through a coarse kitchen strainer. Hold the basket of the strainer approximately ten inches above the blank, and keep it constantly in slow motion while tapping it, to permit even coverage of the blank. This light sifting produces a silver gleam and minute bubbles when fired. If larger bubbles are desired, add larger or thicker flakes with tweezers. In this manner, the size and position of the texture can be controlled.

Calcined forms of mica do not swell, but nevertheless create two-dimensional texture patterns because of their thickness or color. Some flakes are metallic gold in appearance; others granular rather than flat. All are effective when used as the sole means of decoration, but serve equally well as foils for transparent surface colorants.

Fluid glass glazes also cause bubbling when laminated, but for a different reason. The fluid agitates any trapped air after fusion of the glass edges takes place, and such bubbling can be controlled only by varying the amount or thickness of the coating. Since the exact thickness of an applied liquid is difficult to judge, it is virtually impossible to predict size and placement of bubbles, and use of this technique is generally reserved for haphazard backgrounds which will not conflict with surface design.

Sand and the granular carbides position well, with little or no movement on the lower blank. Although these are apt to be drab in color, there is some iridescence, the amount depending on the geographical source of the material. Containing some silica, or composed entirely of silica, sand may be combined with, or sprinkled on, glass glazes, although any iri-

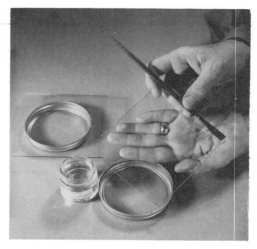

Fig. 36. A band of oil is brushed on the lower blank . . .

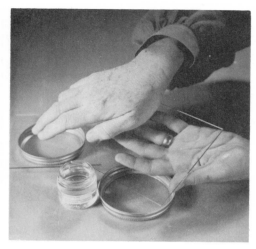

Fig. 37. . . . oil is distributed on the blank with the palm of the hand . . .

Fig. 38. . . . mica flakes are sifted through a coarse strainer . . .

Fig. 39. . . . the lower blank is positioned on the mold . . .

Fig. 40. . . . and then the upper blank is placed on the lower.

Fig. 41. The fired dish.

descence tends to disappear. The glass glazes bubble less when combined with sand.

Bird gravel (a pure form of coarse sand), and table salt—at least the varieties I have tested—retain the original opaque white form.

ENAMELED GLASS

Granular copper enamels are made to function in accordance with the natural performance of the metals to which they are fused. In normal enameling procedure, they are placed in kilns which have been preheated to approximately 1500°F. The coefficients (i.e., expansion when heated; contraction on cooling) of enamel and metal are equal, or nearly so, thus effecting fusion. Sheet glass, as a base for enamel techniques, cannot be subjected to the thermal shock of rapid heating and cooling, nor does it have the coefficient of enamel; consequently this material requires special handling.

The inequality between enamels and glass causes sections of the enamel coating to separate from the base glass in a way comparable to ceramic crackle glazes on clay bodies, and so presents

Fig. 42. A laminated enamel dish. The colors are amethyst and chartreuse. Metallic overglaze outlines the foliage on the surface of the upper blank. (Work of Mrs. Alta Kilts, South Pasadena, Calif.)

a definite problem of adherence. Lamination between two glass blanks secures enamels, although the inequality still sometimes appears as a crackle, which in no way weakens the glass structure itself. Transparent enamels seem to produce this crackle to a greater degree than opaques.

Procedure

Application of enamels to sheet glass parallels that of enamels to copper, with two major exceptions. Since enamels must be confined between two sheets of glass, thickness of enamels should not vary to any great extent, for too great a disparity is apt to shift the upper glass blank as it bends, resulting in misalignment of the two glass blanks. Organic binders, such as gum tragacanth or arabic, generate fumes which are easily dissipated in the open kiln atmosphere of copper enameling; rising between the glass blanks, these inevitable fumes are often trapped, discoloring both the enamel coating and the glass structure. Although light oils, such as baby oil, are also volatile, there is no solid matter to be consumed, and fumes are greatly diminished.

Brush the oil around the edges of the lower blank, and then distribute it on the entire blank with the palm of your hand. (Paper or cloth distribution would remove the oil.) This procedure makes the oil application even, depositing it on bare areas and lessening the amount brushed on the edges.

Solid Ground Colors

Sift the enamels on the lower blank in the usual enameling procedure;
light or heavy sifting is a matter of personal choice. A contrasting border may be sifted on the first ground color. If a bubbled texture is desired, sprinkle mica flakes sparingly on the layer (or layers) of enamel.

Design Placement

Oil-treat the lower blank as above. Sift simple designs as desired, through a small strainer. For extremely small areas, use an open thimble, with nylon stocking mesh serving as the screen, to control excessive scattering of the enamel granules. Secure the nylon to the thimble with small elastic bands. If, despite control, the granules manage to fall on designated bare areas to some extent, remove them from such areas with a brush or cotton Q-tip between siftings of different colors. Enameled designs can be masked lightly (and carefully) with cardboard, to allow more freedom in sifting adjoining sections.

Although transparent enamels are best suited for emphasizing the transparency or translucency of glass, there are occasions when the addition of opaques strengthens an otherwise indefinite design. Black, applied sparingly, will provide shading and delineate outlines; white is useful for backgrounds and highlighting other colors, although it diminishes the clarity of the glass. An accent of opaque red often vitalizes a nondescript, portrayal. Selection of color is entirely a matter of design and personal choice. I do not intend in this section to instruct in the fundamentals of design, but rather to describe the inherent characteristics of glass

Fig. 43. The lower blank is oiled, the enamel border sifted.

Fig. 44. Opaque white ceramic frit is lightly sifted on the center.

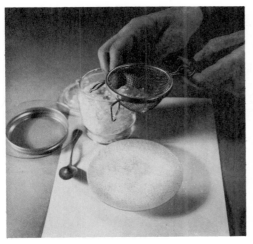

Fig. 45. Mica flakes are added to the enamel and the frit.

Fig. 46. The finished plate.

Fig. 47. A set of enameled plates and a bowl.

Fig. 48. Other enameled pieces. The larger dish has black and gold decal fired on its surface.

Fig. 49. The blank is oiled, then black enamel is sifted . . .

Fig. 50. . . . turquoise enamel is sifted within the black outlines . . .

Fig. 51. . . . yellow enamel is overlaid on the turquoise . . .

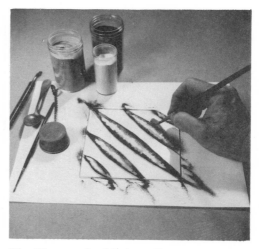

Fig. 52. . . . the black outlines are straightened with a brush . . .

Fig. 53. . . . and the raised ridges of enamels are tamped with a tool.

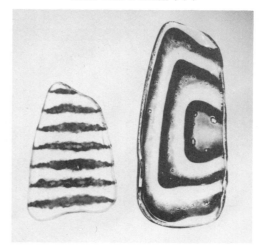

Fig. 54. Two fired examples of enameled design.

and enamels and, more importantly, to stress the reactions of one to the other, so that reasonably accurate results become predictable.

Do not assume that enamels invariably retain original coloration; combination with glass often alters certain shades. Strong, clear greens are apt to take on a bluish cast; most pinks become rather purple; one opaque purple fires to a surprising fuchsia. For the most part, garnets, cobalt blues, and browns change very little in lamination. The serious craftsman will run tests on each enamel he plans to use, for future reference.

Fig. 55. A simple pattern of a ship is sketched on both paper and glass blank. The blank is then oiled. Foil is placed between the pattern and the tissue paper; the sail and the hull are cut out with small scissors.

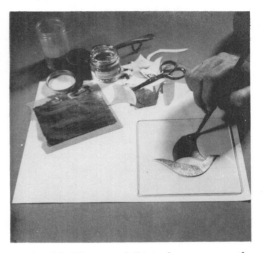

Fig. 56. The cut foil sections are gently transferred to the blank, and smoothed with an oiled brush.

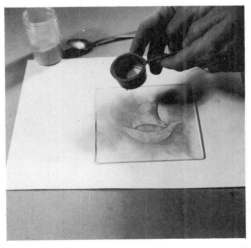

Fig. 57. Then transparent garnet enamel is lightly sifted on the foil and the surrounding blank area.

Fig. 58. The foil is highlighted by removing enamel with the brush in curving strokes. (Silver foil appears as gold under fired transparent red enamels; thus, highlighting shows both gold and silver effects.)

51

Fig. 59. Drapery fabric: the over-all pattern consists of a white background, with dull green, maroon, and gray designs accented with black and metallic gold. The center of the illustration shows preliminary sketches executed in water color.

Fig. 60. An individual design unit is selected and sketched directly on both blanks with a graphite pencil for glass. Allowance for the leaf is indicated on the upper blank; curves are reversed, since the decorated blank will be placed face down upon the lower blank, thus sealing the juxtapositioned underglaze applications within the two glass blanks. Background lines are also sketched on the lower blank.

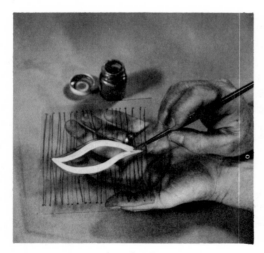

Fig. 61. *Decorating the lower blank:* Blue underglaze is brushed with broad strokes.

Fig. 62. The inner portion receives light gray brush strokes; the lines are dark gray.

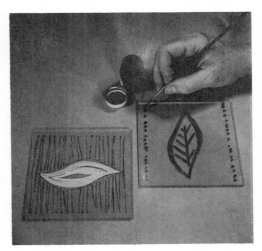

Fig. 63. *Decorating the upper blank:* Foliage green is applied as a border of the leaf, serving to emphasize the lighter colors.

Fig. 64. Black dots and veins are then added.

Fig. 65. **The upper blank is placed on the lower. The black dots now become the terminal points for the linear background of the lower blank; the veining corresponds to the shape of the leaf. Gold metallic overglaze is applied to the surface of the upper blank.**

Fig. 66. Designs of the preliminary sketches shown in Fig. 59 after firing. All four were executed according to the above procedure.

Fig. 67. Plate: underglaze lamination. This features brush strokes of coral, jade, and chartreuse translucent ceramic underglaze. The outlining is of black underglaze.

Combination with Other Decorating Mediums

Any technique of laminated enameling can often be combined with those pertaining to other materials, to good advantage.

Silver and gold foils for enameling can be affixed to the glass surface in the traditional manner prescribed for copper enameling, followed by a light sifting of transparent enamel.

Fiberglass threads and gold or silver mica flakes may be positioned on the enamel application before placement of the top glass blank.

The subsurface: The laminated blanks can be fired over copper wire shapes, placed on a mold which has been coated with a separator. (For details, see section on Wire Indentation.) This technique, of course, would conflict with detailed enamel design, and is suitable only for monotone enamel grounds.

Stained glass transparency "Madonna and Child." Individual sections are grouted to colorless panel. Wrought iron frame.

Free-form shapes are bound with wire; overlapping segments create additional colors. The unit is suspended by wires drawn through the frame.

Lamp. Stained glass fragments are fused to expanded metal panels. Finial is a bottle stopper filled with crushed glass. Wrought iron stands support turquoise base plate and fixture.

Standing owl. Four layers of overlapping glass segments, cut to conform to outline pattern. Heavy copper wire extends from the center of the laminated glass. This was bent after firing to form stand. Colored with glass glaze.

At Left: Free-form bowl of heavy chunk flint glass, covered with glass glaze. Center: Laminated bowl—enamels and mica texture flakes. At Right: Sailboat—laminated glass glaze.

Architectural window panel—stained glass geometric segments fused to colorless seedy glass panel.

Suspension—bird of rose and cobalt stained glass; copper wire scrolls are laminated by extra wing and eye sections.

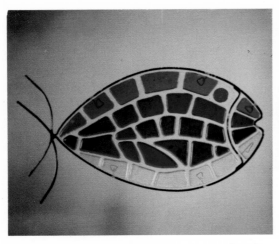

Suspension—stained glass fired on seedy glass panels, wires laminated between panels.

Enamels and sterling wires laminated in glass sections. Wire extensions bind sections to frame.

Standing birds—plate glass with superimposed wings laminating wire stands. Glass glaze coloring.

Two suspensions—figures are formed by overlapping fragments of stained glass.

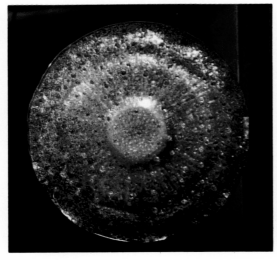

Crystal bowl, colored glass glaze. Texture given by random scattering of crushed glass.

Hanging panel of stained glass. Butterfly design formed by firing panel over heavy wires.

Self-contracting glass gold can be applied to any glass subsurface; whether its use with enamels would become over-ornamentation is a matter of personal discretion.

Surface: Any decorating materials suitable for glass surfaces can be added to emphasize the enameled unit of blanks. Metallic overglazes (gold, platinum, bronze, etc.) applied to the surface of the top blank call attention to the thickness of the glass; the enamel consequently appears to have great depth.

Transparent surface colorings, such as glass glaze and glass lusters, are useful in muting enamel shades for exact matching of draperies, upholstery materials, ceramic tile, or other fixed furnishings.

Enamel "ices" may be applied to glass surfaces, indicating a processing perhaps similar to that of enamel threads. To date, the range of available colors is not as extensive as that of the traditional enamels for copper. Further experimentation is necessary before a complete evaluation can be given. Certainly there are great possibilities indicated, which should prove an inspiring challenge to the craftsman with an inquisitive mind.

LAMINATION OF CERAMIC UNDERGLAZE

Articles and treatises have been written which stress the use of underglazes on clay bodies and techniques which depend on absorbency of the liquid content of these colorants by greenware or bisque have also received much attention. Underglazes may be successfully laminated, if it is borne in mind that glass has an impervious rather than a porous surface, and that prolonged manipulation of any water-soluble medium inevitably results in puddles of mixed color, rather than discernible design. However, since most prepared underglazes contain a surface hardener (or binder), it is possible to apply them rapidly without retouching. When the first applications are dry, contrasting color can be added as shading by employing light, sure strokes. Underglaze, whether background effect, linear, or shaded design, is always executed on the surface of the lower blank in lamination. Underglazes, as the name implies, are calcined pigments which retain coloration at firing temperatures, but depend on a protective covering of transparent glaze (on clay bodies) to develop the colors. Although the upper glass blank provides a coating, it does not deepen or change specific shades of underglaze. Therefore, select the colors as they appear in the bottles.

Squeegee Patterns

In addition to the usual techniques of applying underglaze, such as linear, brush stroke, sponging, and spraying, there is a method of design adaptable only to glass.

Spontaneous patterns can be created by painting a desired underglaze on the surface of the lower blank, and while it is still wet, positioning the upper blank to correspond with the contour of the lower. Then "swivel" the upper blank about 90 degrees to the right or left, return to the original placement, and separate the two

Fig. 68. "Skyline Scene." Colors of plaza and buildings: green, yellow, blue, lavender, and pink translucent ceramic underglaze. Watercolor technique on lower blank. The outlining is of black underglaze, executed on the sub-surface of the upper blank. (The pattern was reversed to place the outlining within the two sheets of glass.)

blanks. A considerable vacuum results, and the separation of the blanks is sometimes a little difficult. Wipe clean the edges of the two blanks with a damp cloth to approximately ¼″ from the outer edge, as the underglaze often "boils" between the blanks during the firing, and it can overflow onto the mold.

When both sections are dry, place them together again, and fire the laminated pieces. This technique results in strange and wonderful patterns on both upper and lower blanks, and is an adventure resembling the ink-blot tests given in appraisal of personality. No two patterns can ever be duplicated. Coral branch formations, delicate leaf veinings, webbing, and sometimes a series of shadowy dots are a few of the designs caused by varying the consistency and thickness of the underglaze application. Thin coatings produce delicate patterns; puddles which are poured instead of painted, form into bold and larger motifs. Separated or spaced background designs are obtained by using small circles (flashlight lenses will do nicely), triangles, or strips of scrap glass, manipulated in the same manner as the entire blank. Each glass shape seems to devise a distinctly characteristic imprint.

Where cloudy or irregular backgrounds are desired for other design techniques, underglazes may be stippled or sponged on the lower blank, whether the subsequent design is to be executed in underglaze or some other medium. As a rule, translucent underglazes are more brilliant and intense than the flat or opaque variety.

Other materials may be used in conjunction with underglaze designs, thus evolving entirely new techniques. The following suggestions have proved to be satisfactory adjuncts to underglaze lamination:

Enamels

Enamels for copper can be sifted on any bare areas of the lower blank. This is especially useful for borders surrounding the design. Cover the design with a shield of paper or cardboard to prevent blurring by scattered

Fig. 69. Earrings—matching dress fabric.

granules of enamel. Be sure the underglaze is dry before placing the shield.

Mica Texture Flakes

Silver or gold texture flakes may be added sparingly on the underglaze design for sparkle, if such use is consistent with, and does not obliterate, the design. For example, black or dark blue backgrounds suggest night scenes when the texture flakes are used as "stars"; a few flakes create the illusion of bubbles for an undersea effect.

Metallic Overglaze

Touches of liquid glass gold on the surface of the *upper* blank brighten or delineate weak and indefinite designs, and also provide a three-dimensional effect. The sketch for the underglaze design is also used for the gold accents; in this way, placement of the gold synchronizes perfectly with the design. The gold should be dried overnight before firing. Greater depth is achieved by using thick glass for both blanks.

Fig. 70. The lower blank is brushed with translucent underglaze.

Fig. 71. The upper blank is placed on the lower and swiveled in a one-quarter turn . . .

Fig. 72. . . . the blanks are separated . . .

Fig. 73. . . . and the edges are cleaned. After drying, the blanks are placed together again, the underglazed sides facing one another.

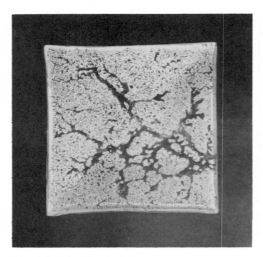

Fig. 74. The fired dish.

Fig. 75. Spot stamping of the underglaze, and the glass shapes used.

Fiberglass Threads

Fiberglass threads, unraveled from draperies or yard goods, may be brushed with underglaze on all sides and coiled into abstract patterns on the lower blank. Fine lines of color are thus controlled without evident weakness.

Liquid Glass Colors

Transparent glass glazes can be applied to the surface of the upper blank. An intermediate color often blends two unrelated shades of the underglaze design below, as well as softening harsh colors. Pale underglaze colors, on the other hand, are strengthened by a medium application of glass glaze to the top blank. This application, like the glass gold accents, creates an effect of depth in the fused unit.

Excess application of underglaze can check and separate into fissures, as well as create trapped air. This defect raises a portion of the upper blank following the design outline and extends approximately ⅛″ to ½″, depending on the thickness of the glass.

Underglaze must be dry before firing, to prevent discoloration and frostiness caused by condensation.

Pressure on, or retouching of design, whether wet or dry, invariably releases previous applications of underglaze, which adhere to the brush.

LAMINATION OF METALS: SCREEN

Although copper oxidizes and gradually diminishes in thickness if fired many times, copper screen disintegrates less than other metal meshes when sealed by lamination. It provides a less definite pattern than solid forms such as the lightweight metal foils, and is useful as a subordinate accent when planned as an adjunct to color, or when a semirigid strength for a panel is indicated. Generally the fired appearance is black, due to the inevitable oxidation, although a lighter firing may preserve some of the original color. Processing of certain brands in which the screen is coated with a preservative also tends to retain the copper look.

To return to the original premise: there should be a reason for the lamination of any material and the justification must also include careful consideration of the individual characteristics of any material in relationship to the known reactions of the encasing glass. It is evident that broad statements can be contradictory and often misleading. For example, it is completely true that metal screen can be laminated between two sheets of glass. At this point, however, unless there is some amplification of the statement, end or fired results can prove to be disastrous, for it is the selection of the project itself which is the crux of the situation. Glass is flexible when subjected to heat; metals are less so. The combination of the two is successful only when the limitations of the metal are recognized. Fired flat, screen and glass are in perfect harmony, each undergoing its individual reaction independently. Attempts to enforce a three-dimensional shape by bending into a mold or over a protuberance

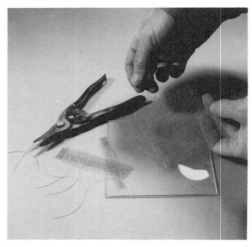

Fig. 76. Copper screening is cut ½ inch smaller than the blank; the edges are fringed by removing strands of wire.

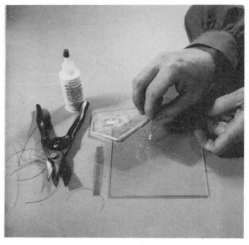

Fig. 77. The fringed screen is glued to the lower blank.

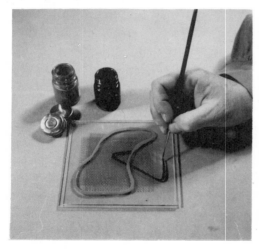

Fig. 78. The upper blank is placed over the lower; translucent underglaze design is added.

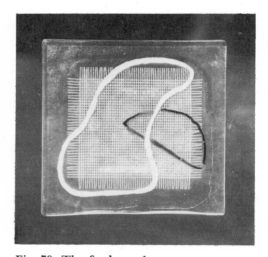

Fig. 79. The fired panel.

abruptly terminate the harmony, for the glass will try to conform to the contour of the model, and the screen will not. This conflict usually fractures the glass. The craftsman must therefore evaluate not only the glass and the substance to be laminated, but should also study the structure on which the combination is to be fired. The following suggestions may be helpful:

Flat-Fired Panels

1. Screen and glass may be of the same dimensions for a flat-fired panel.

2. Screen may extend beyond the glass panel for structural purposes when post-fired panels indicate such installation (see section on panels for concrete blocks).

3. Screen shapes may be cut with tin snips or shears, and utilized as decorative elements of design between

60

full-sized blanks, or layers of adjoining glass segments.

Bent Glass

Screen shapes may be positioned on areas that will assume a flat surface after the blanks have been fired. Since bent firings can vary slightly, depending on placement of the mold in the kiln and the speed with which the firing progresses, positioning of the screen is at best merely approximate, but an adequate marginal allowance around the screen shape usually compensates for slight irregularities in the sagging. If, after close study of the problem you are still undecided, it would be wise to fire two blanks of identical thickness and size with the ultimate project to ascertain the fired formation. If the planned position of the screen can be delineated with underglaze on the upper surface of the lower blank, exact placement for subsequent firings can be determined.

As metals have a chemical reaction to certain colorants, it is generally more satisfactory to fire them between

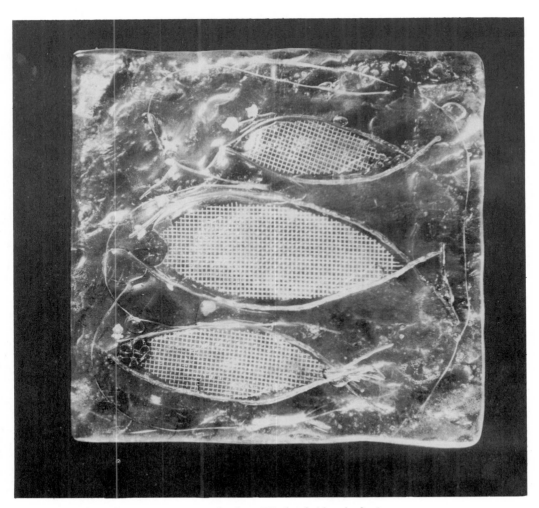

Fig. 80. Laminated copper screen and wire. (Work of Alta Andre.)

bare blanks, reserving coloration of the glass for the upper exposed surface of the top blank. Dry materials such as enamel or ceramic frits are apt to clog screen mesh, obscuring the pattern even if there is no chemical reaction, and liquids, of course, create moisture and often emit discoloring fumes within the blanks.

LAMINATION OF METALS: WIRE

Wire, fine or heavy gauge, may be laminated for purposes of design, or it may serve in a functional capacity, usually as a means of suspending free-floating glass shapes within a frame.

Metals oxidize when exposed to the atmosphere—such light oxidation is described as tarnishing. Subjected to heat, metal oxidation is more pronounced, some metals producing a detachable layer known as "scale" or "fire scale." Fine wire forms less scale than heavy gauge wire, simply because there is less surface area to be oxidized. With the possible exception of sterling silver and some grades of

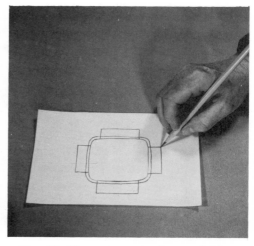

Fig. 81. The size and shape of the block opening is penciled on paper.

Fig. 82. The pattern is decreased (shown by the inner line), and the extension of the screen is indicated.

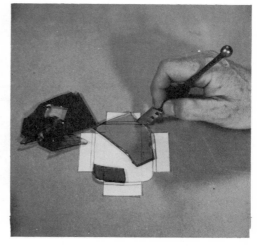

Fig. 83. Copper screen is taped to the pattern, and cut out with tin snips.

Fig. 84. Segments of cathedral glass are roughly cut. (The outer edges must not exceed the decreased pattern.)

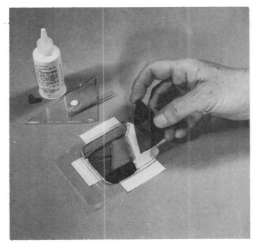

Fig. 85. Flexible sheet plastic is taped over the pattern; the segments are glued to the plastic.

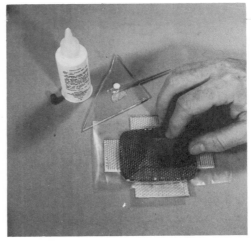

Fig. 86. The screen cut-out is glued to the layer of glass segments.

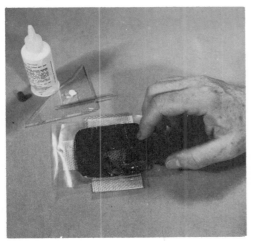

Fig. 87. An additional layer of glass is glued to the screen; the joinings in the second layer overlap those of the first layer.

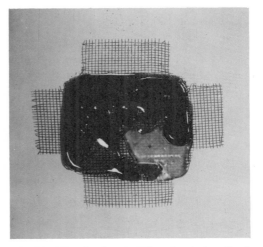

Fig. 88. The fired unit. The plastic has fired out . . . the screen is now laminated.

Fig. 89. The extending screen flaps are folded back at right angles.

Fig. 90. The panel is inserted into the block opening.

63

Fig. 91. Water is added to ready-mix cement to a stiff consistency, then the cement is troweled over the screen flaps with a spatula.

Fig. 92. When set, the cement is textured with a wire brush to conform to the block.

Fig. 93. The completed block.

nichrome, oxidation to any degree presents a black appearance when laminated. This predictable transformation can be utilized as an integral part of a planned design. For formal designs add a pencil sketch to the paper pattern used for cutting the glass blanks, thus preserving specifications of the proposed project for reference. Shape the wire section or sections by hand or with tools, to corre-

spond with the sketch. When the selected shapes have been formed, place the blank over the sketch for positioning of the wire. To eliminate the possibility of displacement, affix the wires to the base blank with a small dot of glue at strategic points. Unless the wire conforms to the glass, place a weight on the entire design until the glue hardens enough to hold the wire in place. Needle-nose and round-jaw pliers are useful in shaping wires, and end-wire cutters sever the wire without distorting the shapes.

Preheating (annealing) copper wire to at least 1000°F. serves a dual purpose: the annealing renders it more pliable, and fire scale forming on annealed wire is less apt to scatter within the glass when laminated. On the other hand, annealing nichrome or Kanthal is definitely detrimental, since these wires become rigid and unyielding when prefired, making them difficult if not impossible to shape.

It is generally wiser to add any colorants or other decorating me-

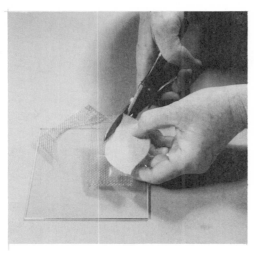

Fig. 94. The shape is designed within the limits of the flat bottom of the ultimate bent plate, and sketched on paper. The pattern is taped to the screen, and the screen is cut with tin snips . . .

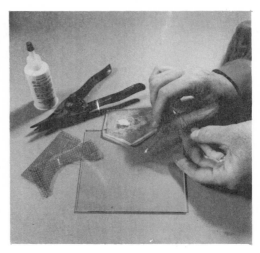

Fig. 95. . . . and glued to the blank.

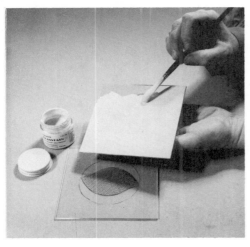

Fig. 96. A penciled line on the blank indicates the circular flat area of the mold. Chartreuse glass glaze is then applied with a brush to the upper blank.

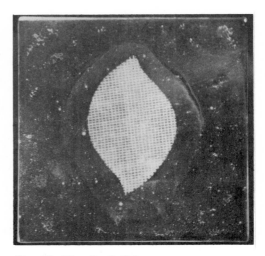

Fig. 97. The fired dish.

diums to the surface of the upper blank, to avoid chemical conflict with the metal wires, and possible obscuring of the design.

Medium gauge wires can be planned as extensions beyond the glass edges to bind fired glass shapes to wire frames (as illustrated in Figure 104).

Heavier gauges, from #12 on, will be rigid enough to install in wooden frames.

PARTIAL LAMINATION

The phrase "partial lamination" means exactly what the two words imply: glass that is only partially lami-

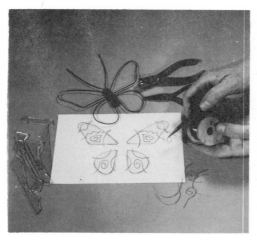

Fig. 98. Two blanks are cut to fit each wing. Fine nichrome wire is shaped to conform with a previously sketched pattern.

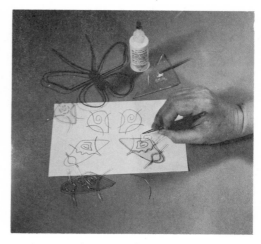

Fig. 99. The lower blanks are placed on the pattern; wires are then glued to the blanks.

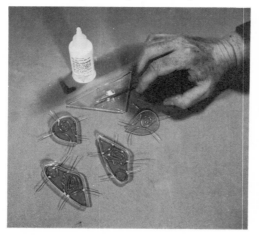

Fig. 100. The upper blanks are glued to the corresponding lower units.

Fig. 101. The fired wing sections are fitted to the frame. Extending wires are bound to the frame with needle-nose jewelry pliers. The ends of the antenna wires are curved with round-nose pliers.

Fig. 102. The completed project.

Fig. 103. Another butterfly, of red cathedral glass. The dark areas are black translucent underglaze.

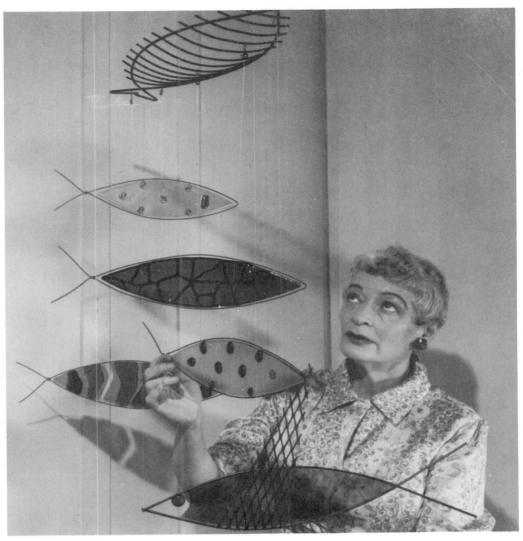

Fig. 104. The author positioning wire-framed glass fish shapes. Fine nichrome wire was laminated and extended beyond the blanks. The extensions were used to bind the glass to the wire frames after firing.

nated. Although superimposing segments of glass can be a purely decorative approach, often the technique is used to perform a utilitarian function.

The addition of precut smaller shapes to the blank is one way of relieving flat or extremely shallow bent forms where no elaborate or obvious design has been planned. Circular disks, squares, rectangles, and triangles can be positioned on the blank as borders, or as individual units. If the shapes are small in relation to the blank, they may be of any thickness, providing that all the shapes are of the same thickness. Varying thicknesses are apt to place a strain on the base. For the same reason, the distribution of the shapes should be com-

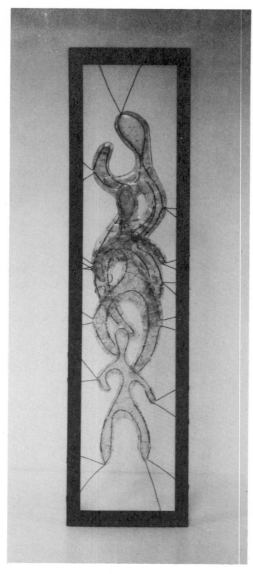

Fig. 105. "Dancing Ghosts." A combination of techniques. Fragmentation (three layers) and lamination of extending wires for suspension in the wooden frame. The surface is colored with purple, blue, turquoise, and emerald glass glaze.

paratively equal. Disproportionate or large shapes of thick glass, particularly when placed irregularly, nearly always fracture the blank. If such shapes are cut from "picture glass" (the thinnest and lightest weight glass available in shops ordinarily supplying window and door glass), there is little strain on the blank, and most projects have been successful.

A variation of the principle of equal weight distribution is the lattice pattern shown in Fig. 118; strips of equal width, length, and thickness are affixed to the blank. Since there is no variation in placement, this arrangement fires satisfactorily, whether the strips are thinner or thicker than the blank.

JEWELING

Loose or unattached jewels of stained glass can be prefired, in exactly the same manner as are jewels of bottle or other glass, with due regard, of course, to the firing temperature of the specific glass and particular type of kiln employed. The properties of stained glass, however, permit the craftsman to by-pass the separate process of prefiring jewels for the glass blank. It is the difference in the fusing temperatures of these two dissimilar types of glass that makes this seeming paradox a feasible technique. The stained glass, having a lower melting point, progresses to the "balling" stage, while the colorless commercial blank is entering the initial discernible phase of the rounding of the vertical edges. Thus, jewels are fully formed *without* a like movement of the glass blank.

Step 1. To ensure jewels of a consistent size, cut even strips of stained glass, the width of the strip determining the size of the jewel. For example, if ¼″ jewels are desired, the cut strips should measure ¼″ in width. This is best accomplished by using graph paper, or by drawing two parallel pencil lines on paper. Place the straight edge of the piece of stained glass exactly on one of the parallel lines, and score and sever the strip as outlined under "Basic Techniques of Sheet Glass"—"Cutting the Glass."

Step 2. Sever square blocks, equal to the width of the strip, either with a glass cutter, or with tile nippers used for cutting mosaic tiles. If you choose the latter method, align the nippers with the strip at a 90-degree angle; otherwise the blocks will be slanting instead of square.

Step 3. Then nip off the corners of each block, to resemble an octagon. This basic shape will ball into a perfectly rounded cabochon when fired; triangles become teardrops in shape; rectangles become ovals.

It is necessary only to glue these rough shapes to the base glass to ensure perfect formative results. Jewels should not touch each other, however,

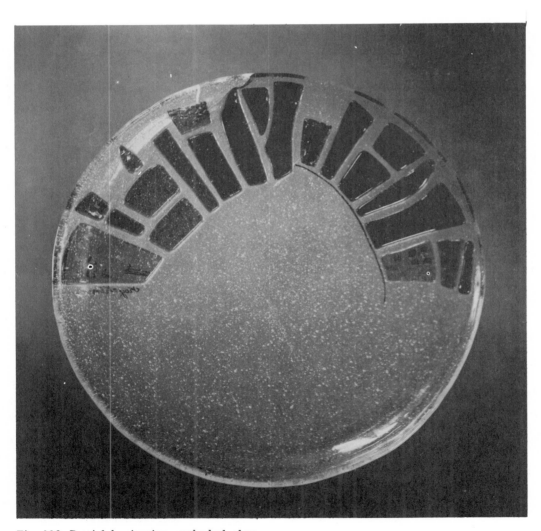

Fig. 106. Partial lamination—cathedral glass.

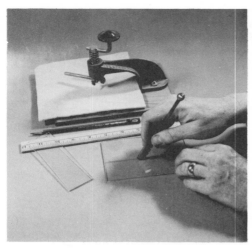

Fig. 107. A lens cutter is shown in the background. Strips of glass are cut. (Removal of margins is allowed for when measuring the width of the strips.)

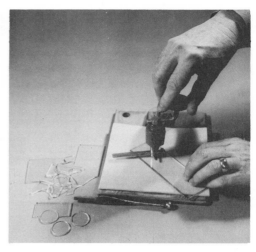

Fig. 108. The strip is positioned under the bar of the cutter. The handle is pressed down to establish contact of the cutting wheel with the glass strip. The circle is scored by rotating the handle.

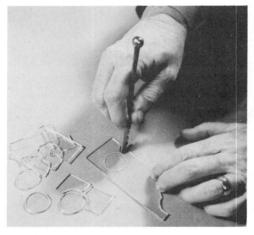

Fig. 109. After establishing cleavage of the disk, radiating lines are scored from the disk to the edge, then tapped to remove the margin in sections. See general glass cutting.

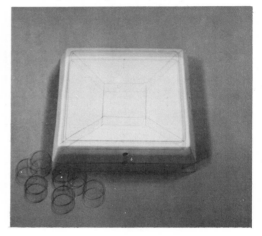

Fig. 110. The blank is positioned on the penciled mold.

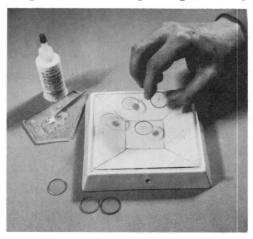

Fig. 111. The disks are glued to the blank, avoiding mold angles.

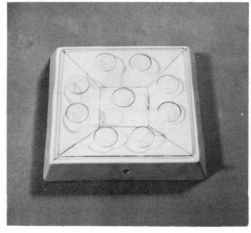

Fig. 112. The completed blank. The glued disks will not be distorted by bending of the blank at the mold edges.

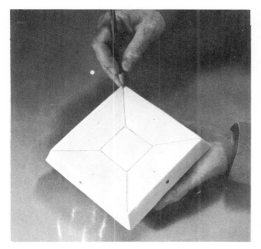

Fig. 113. Angles of the mold are penciled . . .

Fig. 114. . . . narrow strips are severed (graph paper was used as a cutting pattern) . . .

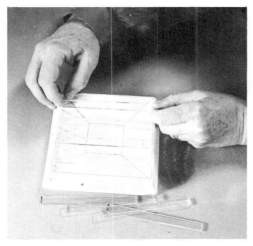

Fig. 115. . . . the glass blank is placed on the mold. Four strips are glued at spaced intervals . . .

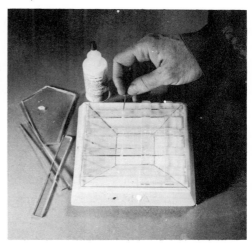

Fig. 116. . . . and the remaining four strips are added across the lower row.

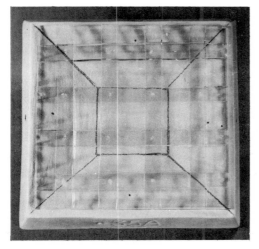

Fig. 117. The "latticed" blank is ready to be fired.

Fig. 118. The fired dish, and an openwork bowl. The apparent distortion of the latter is due to firing in a deep mold.

Fig. 119. Parallel lines of the selected width of the blocks are sketched on paper. Strips are cut; the blocks are severed with small nippers.

Fig. 120. Straight lines on the blank pattern indicate placement of the blocks.

Fig. 121. The blank is laid on the pattern. Various shades of blue and green blocks are then glued to the blank, according to the pattern. The blocks are separated by approximately ¼ inch.

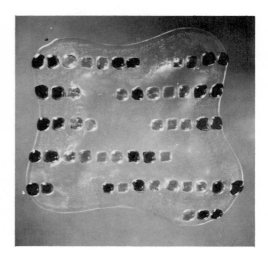

Fig. 122. The fired dish.

since two or more would tend to establish a new glass structure inconsistent with the reaction of the base glass. When considered as individual units, each jewel, whether large or small, can pass through the preliminary cycles. Glue should be absolutely dry prior to firing, as fresh glue

is apt to cause discoloration or "frost" the entire project.

If the blank is to be bent, study the mold before jeweling. Do not position jewels where the blank will sag from horizontal to vertical planes, but glue them only to areas that will remain horizontal, such as the bottom or the rim of the fired form. Jewels should be omitted from surfaces which will assume a fluted design (cigarette rests on ashtrays, for example), for jeweling would defeat the purpose of such fluting, filling in the depressions.

Suggested Projects for Jeweling Blanks

Panels for light fixtures.

Clock dials, the jewels marking the hours; or in the case of very large dials, minutes may be designated by jewels smaller than the hour indicators.

Christmas ornaments.

Jewelry.

Decorative hanging suspensions.

Any bent piece where such jeweling would not interfere with the function of the project; i.e., a cake plate would not be practical from a serving standpoint, if jeweled.

EXTENSIONS OF WIRE

Partial lamination is employed to secure or encase wire for projects where full lamination would result in excessive weight, or where the superimposed glass is to become a three-dimensional factor of design. Loops can be formed of fine nichrome wire, glued to the blank, and subsequently covered with a symmetrical or asymmetrical segment of glass, only slightly larger than the size of the loop. This technique is a favorite for jewelry, Christmas ornaments, and similar small suspensions, especially when equipment for drilling holes is unavailable. As the size of the suspension increases, the wire should be correspondingly heavier to provide ade-

quate strength. Hairpins have proved satisfactory for medium projects; generally, 16- or 18-gauge wire loops will suffice for glass weighing up to a pound. The covering glass segment should be considerably larger for the heavy wire, to ensure complete encasement.

Wires may extend beyond the blank and superimposed glass, as the means of attaching the glass to a wire frame. Two examples are shown: the wire forms a lineal portion of the fish structure; extension of the wire approximately one inch permits post-fired installation. The butterfly was similarly planned, the encasing glass

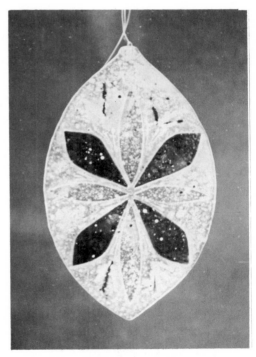

Fig. 123. Christmas ornament (partial lamination). Superimposed shapes of picture glass were glued to the blank. It was then colored with blue and green glass glaze, and bits of glass and enamel flakes were added for texture. (Work of Shirley Kane Wilson, Covina, Calif.)

73

Fig. 124. Nichrome wire is cut into equal lengths; loops are bent at one end. (Loops assure stable lamination of the wire.)

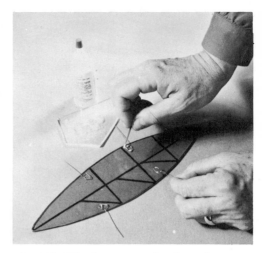

Fig. 125. The loops are glued at the outer edges of the blank.

Fig. 126. Strips are cut in curves to conform to the fish shape of the blank. Blocks are severed from the strip with a glass cutter . . .

Fig. 127. . . . and glued over the wire loops. Additional segments are added to center section.

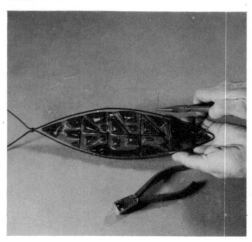

Fig. 128. After firing, the extending wires are wrapped several times around a wire frame.

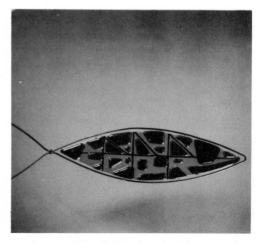

Fig. 129. The finished unit. The space between the glass and the frame permits the addition of nylon fishing line for suspending the unit.

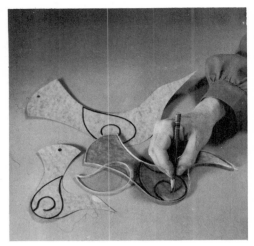

Fig. 130. Wing and wire placement is indicated in ink on the paper patterns. The bird blank is placed on the cut-out pattern; wing and wire placement is traced on the blank with glass pencil.

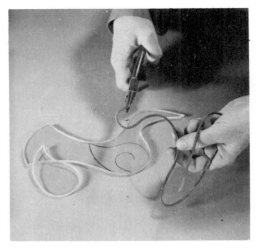

Fig. 131. Then annealed heavy wire is curved to correspond with the pattern . . .

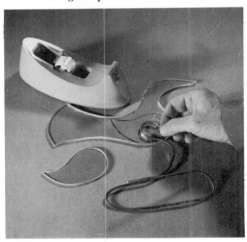

Fig. 132. . . . the curved end is cellophane-taped to the blank . . .

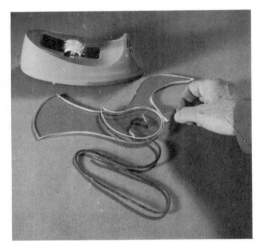

Fig. 133. . . . the wing section is cellophane-taped to the blank and wire unit . . .

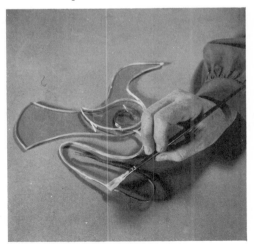

Fig. 134. . . . and the extending wire is coated with separator.

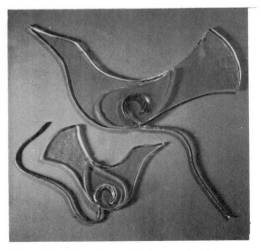

Fig. 135. Two fired birds, ready for any desired technique of decorating.

75

in this instance being colored glass buttons.

Extensions of wire to form supporting stands for glass must be even heavier than that used for suspended projects. The plate glass birds required 10-gauge copper wire to sustain the extreme weight of the glass.

Fig. 136. A standing cross. Fragmentation of shards, with heavy wire extensions for the stand.

D. DECORATING TECHNIQUES

SURFACE

The surface of certain brands of color-less commercial glass can be effectively patterned by painting desired areas with a 50% solution of silicate of soda (half water, and half silicate of soda as it is purchased in liquid form at drugstores). Completely colorless, and difficult to see while being brushed, it may be tinted with food coloring, which burns out in the firing. As silicate of soda is a form of glass, the logical conclusion is that chemical reaction between the two diverse glass compounds takes place, resulting in a dull finish, somewhat resembling ground glass. As is the case with most water-soluble liquids, silicate of soda is not feasible for delicate detail, but produces bold, broad designs excellently. The contrast between the dull and glossy areas is pleasant, if nebulous. (Memo: On colors and brands of stained glass I have tested, no trace of the silicate of soda remained after firing.)

TEXTURE: GLASS CRUSHINGS

The small bits left over from the cutting of sheet glass blanks can be used for texture, providing that they are clean. Although these fine particles soften earlier than the thicker sheet glass, they never become fluid

Fig. 137. Application of glass glaze begins in the center of the blank.

Fig. 138. As additional glaze is added, the brush strokes overlap and radiate outward . . .

Fig. 139. . . . until the blank is entirely covered.

Fig. 140. The vertical edges are then cleaned.

Fig. 141. Crushed glass (colored and color-less) is scattered on the moist glaze.

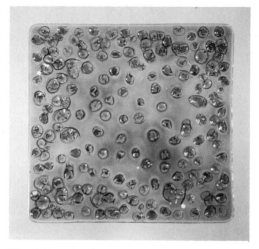

Fig. 142. The fired piece.

at bending temperatures, and therefore create texture of the surface in varying degrees. The larger shards, of course, are more three-dimensional than fine crushings.

If applied to bare glass, crushings should be affixed by oiling the surface (see procedure for ceramic frits). Sprinkled or sifted on a moist surface colorant, no further adhesive is necessary. Since the crushings are also glass, they are usually tinted by the colorant. (Exceptions: lusters and other metallic overglazes.)

To produce extra crushings, if the amount accumulated from cutting is not sufficient:

Heat the glass in a kitchen oven, electric broiler, or directly on an electric hot plate, until it is too hot to be touched by the bare hands. Then remove it with tongs and drop it immediately into a pan of water. Cold water causes a rather large fracturing; ice water results in a fine network crackle. It will cool rapidly, and should again be removed from the water with tongs, and placed to dry on paper or cloth toweling.

When dry, put the pieces in a clean iron skillet and smash them with a hammer. Place the skillet in a plastic bag, to prevent glass bits from scattering. The plastic bag should be large enough to permit the hammer movement, and the hammer should have a fairly broad head. One excellent type for this purpose is used by automotive body repair shops, although there are many other types which may be used.

Crushings can be used in a great many ways: as borders on bare or decorated glass; for filling apertures in clay grilles; as a bonding agent between layers of glass or glass segments, where wire or expanded metal separates the glass to the extent that full contact is dubious; they may be used exclusively for wire or metal strip designs which cannot practically enclose other formations of glass.

Colored sheet glass crushings should be pulverized and stored in boxes or jars for selection.

TEXTURE: SAND

Pure, clean sand, being silica, can be sprinkled on such colorants for glass surfaces as will fuse to the glass. For the most part, natural silica is resistant to the heat specified for sheet glass fusion, and lacks cohesion to the glass at these temperatures. It is necessary that bonding be effected by a lower-temperature melting material.

TEXTURE: THE CARBIDES

Silicon and other carbide compounds may also be sprinkled on glass colorants, although they are extremely harsh and unpleasant to the touch. They are generally reserved for wall panels featuring design characteristics which require minute pinpoints as accent, such panels or murals being viewed from a distance, rather than handled.

FULL COVERAGE COLORANTS
Basic Procedure

Since the object of this book is to encourage the craftsman to work with glass as a raw material, manipulating and transforming it toward the development of his own preconceived design (within inherent limitations), only those colorants which mature simultaneously with the firing of the glass are stressed. For the sake of expediency I have restricted decorating to media which respond to a single firing, and have a coefficient (rate of expansion and contraction) similar to the glass. These two stipulations narrow the list of colorants to some extent, but for the most part, each is capable of diversity according to your own imagination and skill.

LUSTERS AND GLAZES

Glass lusters, applied properly, attain complete transparency when fired to the temperatures required for fused glass: 1400° to 1550°F. The lusters are meant to be fired at a much lower temperature, and since any luster color invariably fires to either a pink or lavender shade at this higher degree, due to gold content, remember to select them only when you want these two colors.

Lusters are part of the overglaze field, which has as one main characteristic the complete lack of fluidity. Lusters, liquid metals, and pigments for china painting are actually platings, as distinguished from ceramic glazes which become fluid under heat. Although lint, loose bristles from brushes, and fine particles of foreign matter may burn out, small spots of bare glass result. Most overglazes are prepared with some sort of viscous bonding agent, for easier application on glossy surfaces, but which attracts lint and other airborne matter. For these reasons, it is evident that the glass blank must be scrupulously clean, and that lusters should be applied in a working area with as few air currents as possible.

Lusters dry quickly, and rapid application is a vital factor. Best results are obtained by using a square brush of the "shader" type, which should be of the finest quality, to eliminate loose hairs in the luster coating.

Lusters must be of a flowing consistency to avoid streakiness, and should be applied in an extremely thin coating, which is most easily executed by a series of short, broad strokes, covering small areas. Adjoining sections can be quickly blended in with the brush if the previously applied luster is still fluid enough to intermix. Where adjacent applications show overlapping brush marks, a different procedure must be adopted: as each section becomes tacky, it can be "padded" with a pad of lamb's wool enclosed in china silk, extending the operation well into the newly applied luster. Padding consists of lightly patting the sticky coating, turning the pad slightly as soon as the china silk shows absorption of the luster.

The lustered glass may be fired after 30 minutes' drying time. From a practical viewpoint, immediate firing is desirable. If the blank must be reserved for a future firing, it should be stored in a clean box.

A wide selection of colors is available in a type of "stain" for glass. A water-mixed form of pure transparent glass which fuses satisfactorily to col-

Fig. 143. The blank is cleaned thoroughly with alcohol solvent.

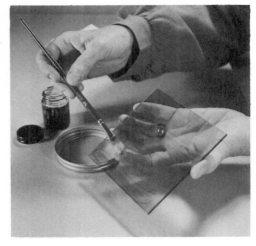

Fig. 144. Glass luster is applied evenly and sparingly.

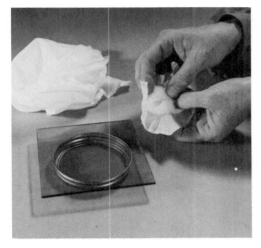

Fig. 145. The pad is prepared by enclosing lamb's wool in china silk.

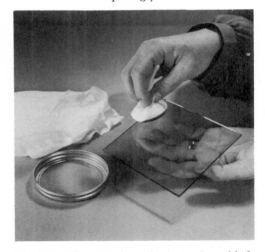

Fig. 146. When "tacky," the luster is padded,

Fig. 147. . . . and the padded blank is stored in a dust-free box.

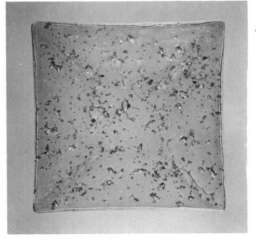

Fig. 148. The fired dish. The texture was achieved by sprinkling mica flakes on the separator-covered mold before bending the blank.

Fig. 149. The predominating color is applied at random . . .

Fig. 150. . . . and a second color is added to some bare areas.

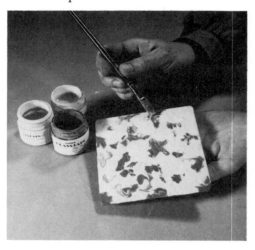

Fig. 151. The darkest color fills in the remaining unglazed spaces.

Fig. 152. The fired dish.

Fig. 153. Two bowls.

Fig. 154. A free-form plate.

Projects shown on this page utilize transparent glass glaze.

orless glass is supplied in liquid form for brushwork or spraying.*

Since glass is impervious to most liquids, it cannot absorb moisture contained in prepared decorating materials. Because of this characteristic, water-mixed coatings are easily disturbed by attempts to touch up completed work. Obviously, the techniques employed in glazing clay bodies, based on absorption of moisture by the clay, and accomplished by separate coats, are not feasible for sheet glass. To achieve an even application, let the glass glaze flow from a generously filled brush, exerting only enough pressure to control the direction of the brush. By holding the brush horizontally, radiating from the center of the blank to the edge, and overlapping the brush strokes about ⅛″, adequate and even coverage can be maintained. Vertical edges must be wiped free of glass glaze. A clean cloth suffices if the glaze is still wet; if dry, it is removed with a damp cloth.

Two adjoining colors often blend together to produce a third chromatic tint. Deliberate juxtapositioning can create great brilliance. Intermingling of a pink-brown and a sapphire blue, for instance, results in a royal purple unobtainable by premixing these two colors.

* Several years ago, no fluid colorant for glass which would meet the requirements for transparency as well as those specified for firing, was available. Nearly 14 months of research and experimentation in my laboratory resulted in this product, which was given the name of "Glasstain" ®. Needless to say, additional experimentation on all types of materials is a constant factor in being able to produce the data for this book.

Background patterns are effective and speedily executed. Select two or more harmonious colors for this technique. Dabble the lightest shade on the blank at random, and while the glass glaze is still wet, add a second, contrasting glaze to the bare areas. Being moist, the glazes blend together. Although the glass glaze is applied only to the surface, the fired blank appears to be permeated with color.

Since this glaze is extremely fluid, it is best used as a full coverage colorant, and is not suitable for detailed design. Simple, bold designs can be executed, and in a bent form often produce swirling kaleidoscopic patterns, for the force of gravity plus the thickness of application combine to create varied, exciting spills of color.

OVERGLAZE

Overglazes are pigments intended primarily for the decoration of glazed ceramic bodies. Maximum brilliance and wide range of color is possible because of low firing temperatures, although recommended temperatures pertain to movement of the glaze beneath, rather than to the reaction of the overglaze. Indeed, some strong pinks and purples are actually benefited by a high degree of heat. Overglazes are more closely related to the true enamel field than to ceramic glazes, when fired on glass at full bending temperatures. Some become transparent; others appear translucent to opaque. Brands vary to a certain extent, making impossible an exact description of specific shades, and a positive statement of reaction to glass.

A minimum amount of testing on scrap glass can give you a permanent record of the particular brand or brands selected.

The same general rules of cleanliness, drying, and firing of metallic overglazes, as outlined in the previous section, apply to overglazes, with one exception: the added factor of color calls for special handling and judgment. Fired on a glazed ceramic object, the opacity of the clay or glaze preserves shading and fine individual lines. Applied to the transparent glass, such overglaze techniques are difficult to observe; although the delicate work is still present, transmission of light through the glass renders it nearly invisible to the eye. In other words, it is rather like painting on air, and methods of application should be adjusted to show these colorants to the fullest advantage. Because of this aspect of indistinctness, only the stronger shades should be used.

Prepared with an oil or heavy medium, overglazes usually present no problems of adherence to the glass. Linear design and calculated brush strokes can be emphasized successfully; lines are controlled most easily by filling a fine pointed brush to capacity, and permitting the overglaze to trail onto the glass with little or no pressure. Accent brush strokes by rolling the brush while executing the stroke. The latter technique results in intensified color at one side of the brush stroke. If these manipulations are not familiar to you, a little practice of finger or wrist motions soon brings the desired effect. (Note: Since round brushes appear identical when rolled for sequence photography, I have not attempted to illustrate these brush movements.)

METALLIC OVERGLAZE

Metallic overglazes are pure metals dissolved in such organic vehicles, or carrying agents, as will make them easier to apply. Of themselves, they furnish no gloss, and require a nonporous base for the development of the unfired substance. While firing of metallic overglazes is actually the factor which effects the transmutation, the nature of the surfaces to which they are applied is of prime importance; a glossy base resulting in a polished metallic appearance, and a matte undercoating in a dull finish. Deposited on unfluxed materials, such as clay, the metallics do not develop, and result only in a rather drab purplish stain. Within the ceramic field, familiar undercoatings are glazes on clay bodies, enamels, and glass.

At first glance, the combination of metallics and glass might be considered a dubious choice, for even thin platings of metal are inevitably rigid, and when selected for surface design, indicate probable competition with the inherent sparkle and fragility of glass. Overuse would certainly result in nullification of the very qualities of glass that should be retained. There are, however, instances where transparent contours seem to disappear into the background, or where certain colors lack character. Used sparingly, metallic overglazes can often delineate either an outline of the glass shape, or accentuate indistinct ap-

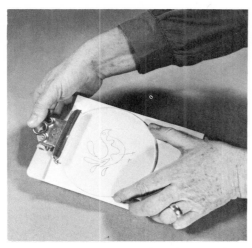

Fig. 155. A simple bird design has been sketched on paper and taped to a clip board. The clamp has been padded with a strip of foam rubber. A round glass blank is clamped over the design.

Fig. 156. The body of the bird is done with bold brush strokes of pink and purple overglaze; the tail feathers are in blue-green and cobalt.

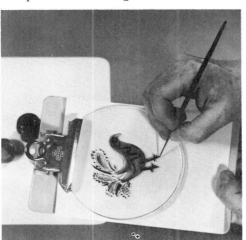

Fig. 157. Black dots enlarge the tail design. The feet, the eye, and the center body scroll are also black.

Fig. 158. Transparent turquoise glass glaze is applied to the edge of the blank.

Fig. 159. The fired design. The blank was fired on a fluted terra-cotta mold.

Fig. 160. Two glass panels with overglaze designs.

Fig. 161. "Family Tree." A combination of techniques. Blue-green enamel and heavy copper wire are laminated between glass leaf shapes. The wire extends for installation. Metallic overglaze was used to inscribe names on the surface of leaves. A driftwood branch was drilled for insertion of the copper wire extensions. The whole was then mounted on a wooden base.

plied design without conflicting with the basic material.

Less obtrusive when applied to the subsurface, metallic designs serve to emphasize the thickness or depth of the glass, and often give the appearance of a thickness greater than the actual measurement. Since metals are opaque, they are perceivable only as dark silhouettes when light is transmitted through the glass; reflected light (from a source in front of the glass object) picks up the gleam of metals. In the latter case, the use of metallic overglaze is invaluable where projects are designed for walls or other opaque backgrounds.

Certain techniques require full me-

tallic backgrounds to stress some particular telic method, such as jeweling, in which case the glass blank becomes subordinate to the ultimate effect, providing only the necessary vehicle for the technique. Ornate heraldic embellishment is but one category that justifies extensive use of metallic overglaze. Thus it is evident that employment of this medium is a matter for personal judgment and prior planning.

Metallic overglazes are usually supplied in liquid form, although some meticulous treatments call for unfluxed metals in paste form. There are numerous formulations; each is prepared for specific co-ordination with the base coating on which it may be superimposed. The fusing points, chemical components, and physical reactions of the undercoatings have a definite bearing on the type of metallic to be selected, hence the array of varieties available.

Since the entire structure of glass softens when subjected to heat, as opposed to the thin base coats of glaze or enamels, metallic overglazes for this specialized branch of ceramics produce far better results than do those for other mediums. The recommended firing temperatures pertain to the characteristics of the object itself, rather than to the metallic with which it is being decorated; thus the concept of "high" or "low" firing in this field is erroneous. The disintegration or burning out of metallics becomes a matter of thin deposits, or more usually, noncohesion with the glass. This is clearly illustrated in the gold category: "ceramic" gold, becoming me-

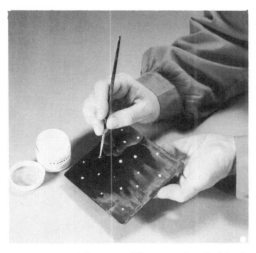

Fig. 162. The metallic overglazed blank was pre-fired to 1000°F. and cooled. Small dots of glass glaze were applied on the gold.

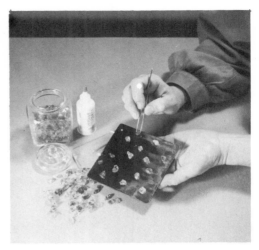

Fig. 163. Glass chunks were glued over the glass glaze dots.

Fig. 164. The fired blank.

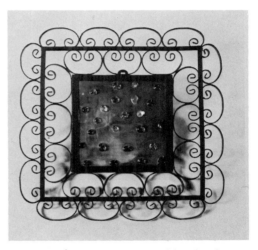

Fig. 165. Installed in a Spanish wire frame.

tallic between 1200° and 1300°F., is apt to discolor or disintegrate on glass at fusing temperatures, whereas "glass" gold, intended for a much lighter firing (in the 960° to 1200°F. range), retains both color and gleam at full glass-bending temperatures of 1375° to 1550°F., thus indicating an affinity for glass. Although the category narrows possible selection to a great extent, there is still a rather bewildering assortment of metallic overglazes for glass, each differing in color-cast or metallic content. The manufacturer generally designates these by numbers rather than by descriptive names.

Gold, platinum, copper, and lusters are available, and these are predictably stable for firing. Some metallics for ceramic decoration can be used where unique effects are desirable and anticipated. Black ceramic luster develops to an antique dark bronze in-

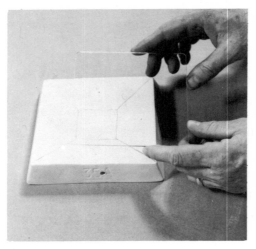

Fig. 166. Angles of the mold are penciled to show the ultimate conformation of the bent piece. The blank is positioned on the mold.

Fig. 167. The mold angles are indicated on the blank.

Fig. 168. The design is sketched on paper and traced on the blank.

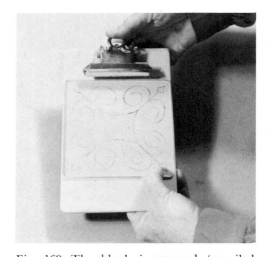

Fig. 169. The blank is reversed (penciled sketch underneath) and clipped to the board.

Fig. 170. The design is executed with liquid glass gold; blank will later be fired on the mold.

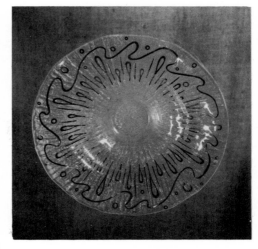

Fig. 171. A crystal and gold bowl.

stead of black; palladium is less mirrorlike on glass, which is perhaps an advantage.

There are certain requirements for successful glass decoration which are applicable to general overglaze techniques. Surfaces must be clean, free from lint, and should receive minimum handling. Due to the viscous organic composition, fumes, smoke, and gases will be emitted during the firing, and these must be expelled or allowed to escape from the kiln, to prevent discoloration or other disfigurement of the glass blank. Metallic overglazes should not be applied to unfired colorants, since the metallic appearance can only be developed on impervious surfaces.

Brushes must be free from residual traces of other decorating media, grease, wax, or foreign matter, for even minute amounts of these can contaminate the sensitive overglazes, resulting in separation of the metal, loss of gleam, bare areas, or discoloration.

Liquid metallic overglazes are usually applied by brushing. Brushes should be soft, flexible, and of high quality to eliminate loosening of hairs or bristles. Since all metallic overglazes result in fired platings rather than fluid dispersal, foreign matter is partially or completely consumed during the firing, leaving bare areas of a like size and shape on the glass. Fine tracery can be executed with a plunger-type tool, the barrel or well of which will hold a considerable amount of liquid. Whether the advantage of "nonstop" application is outweighed by the tedium of empty-

ing the barrel of surplus, and cleaning all movable parts on completing the work, must be a personal decision.

For background effects, the various metallic overglazes can be spattered by dipping the brush in the liquid, then holding it, bristle side down, and drawing a knife or other tool across the bristles. Spraying is possible if gold or luster essence is added to thin the mixture to a consistency that will permit passage through the orifice of the spray gun.

There are several metallic overglaze techniques well known to those familiar with ceramic procedures. They are equally effective on glass, the only changes being a substitution of glass products for ceramic brands, and a due regard for glass firing schedules.

Flotation

Float a few drops of glass gold or glass luster gently on the surface of water, submerge the blank to be decorated at one side (or end) of the container, and remove it slowly at the opposite side. Irregular strata are deposited on the blank, and produce interesting effects when fired. The container of water should be larger than the blank, of course. Prop the blank at a slight angle against a taller object, to drain off the excess water.

Marbleizing

Brush glass gold evenly on the entire surface of the blank with a soft, square shading brush, and allow it to dry. Then apply marbleizing liquid to the gold with as little pressure as possible, and again let the blank dry.

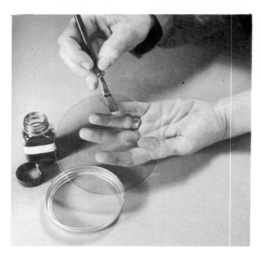

Fig. 172. Self-contracting gold is brushed evenly on the circular blank.

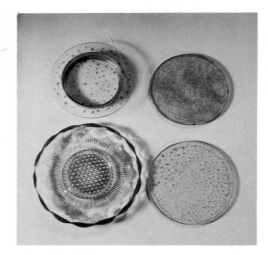

Fig. 173. Different patterns are formed on various types of glass.

Firing of the blank results in a crackled network of the gold. If the subsurface of the blank is treated in this manner, the blank should be prefired, gold side up, to 1000°F., or a slightly tipped cone 022.

Swirled Gold

Apply glass gold thinly as above. When the coating has started to set, but before it becomes tacky, apply marbleizer with rotating brush movement in an allover pattern. Firing brings out a swirling design of gold.

Stamping

Glass gold can be thickened by evaporation (exposure to the air) for a few minutes, until the consistency becomes sticky. It can then be transferred to a rubber stamp, much as regular stamping ink is used, and the design or signature immediately stamped, with slight pressure, on the blank. First deposit the gold on a small piece of glass instead of a stamp pad, and use only a clean, new stamp.

Self-Contracting Gold

One gold compound contracts on drying. Applied evenly but sparingly on a glass surface, drying causes a shrinkage of the coating, resulting in the formation of patterns which leave the glass bare in some areas, concentrated in others. On smooth glass, the formations are generally round in shape, and range from mere specks to good sized dots. Corrugated surfaces produce irregular patches, due to the spreading of the gold into lower levels of the texture while still in a liquid or semiliquid state. I have always thought of this particular compound as "patina gold," for it may be scrubbed into the glass with a stiff brush when tacky and partially dry. Firing produces an over-all burnished patina appearance instead of the usual pattern formations.

Etching of Metallic Overglaze

In addition to the obvious use of metallic overglazes as a decorating medium, they may be combined with

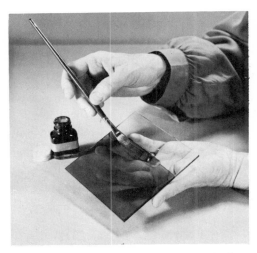

Fig. 174. Metallic overglaze is applied to the blank with a soft, square brush (and is dried; then pre-fired to 1000°F.).

Fig. 175. A simple linear design has been sketched on paper. Glass glaze is flowed on the gold surface according to the prepared design . . .

Fig. 176. . . . and additional colors fill in the unglazed areas.

Fig. 177. The fired blank.

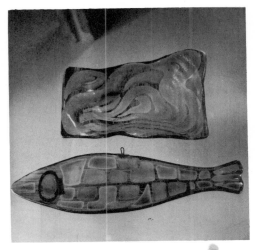

Fig. 178. Fish and bowl. The gold has a burnished look, due to light pre-firing of the blanks.

Fig. 179. Two bent pieces. The gold received harder pre-firing and is more metallic in appearance.

one of the full coverage colorants to create still another technique. During preliminary exhaustive tests of a glass glaze formulated in my laboratories, I discovered that the product attacked metallic overglaze, partially or fully fired, in a corrosive manner, removing the thin plating and at the same time depositing the selected transparent color on the glass base during the ultimate firing. Although this reaction was not deliberately calculated at the outset, it has become a favorite and predictable method for certain types of design.

Fully cover the surface of the glass blank with metallic overglaze, usually gold, although lusters and other metallic platings may be substituted. After drying, fire the blank slowly in a well-vented kiln to 1000°F., or until an 022 cone starts to "tip." The point of firing termination need not be exact, as the light firing of the metallic overglaze results in a dull Roman gold, whereas a slightly harder firing retains a more brilliant shiny metal as a background.

Cool the blank and brush or trail glass glaze on the surface. Since the metallic overglaze is still immature at this point, designing should be freehand without sketching, for penciled marks will cut through the tender coating and perhaps repel the colorant, causing the glaze to withdraw or "crawl" from the sketch. The gold untouched by the glass glaze adheres to the glass in its original appearance, while the fluid colorant etches the design. Heavy application of glass glaze spreads to some extent, hence this technique is not suitable for detailed

work. Two or more colors may be used, either adjoining or separated by areas of the gold, as personal choice dictates. If the gold is to predominate, liberal spacing between the areas of overlaid colorant should be allowed, to compensate for possible spreading.

After the blank dries, it may be fully fired, either as a flat panel, or bent in a mold.

ENAMEL THREADS

Enamel threads, due to their processing, will fuse to the glass surface. Drawn from molten enamel lumps, the threads receive heat sufficient to bring their coefficient closer to that of the glass.

Position the threads on bare glass with glue, for they have a tendency to dislodge during the early stages of firing. They may be added to moist glass glaze, luster, or overglaze coatings, the coatings usually being adhesive enough to secure them without adding glue.

Where there is a limited selection of specific curves or angles in the original manufacturer's packaging, or if perfectly flat shapes are desired, the threads may be flattened by heating in one of the small "hot plate" enamel kilns. Angles and curves can be created or eliminated by manipulating them with long-handled tweezers at the exact moment the threads start to soften. The threads should be heated on sheet mica, or on a piece of sheet brass (or shim) which has been annealed, and must be removed from the heat before they start to spread.

The threads themselves can be

drawn from lump enamels by the following procedure:

A good-sized lump of enamel is rotated (preferably while held with self-locking tweezers) in the flame of a cylinder type butane torch. When the lump softens noticeably on the outside, force a Pyrex glass rod against the exposed surface. Withdrawing the lump quickly from the flame cools it enough to cause it to adhere rigidly to the Pyrex rod. After cooling is complete, rotate the lump and Pyrex rod in the flame, and attach a second glass rod when the lump again softens. The rods should be positioned so that they extend from the lump horizontally, and are perfectly aligned. After cooling to ensure cohesion, again place the unit in the flame and rotate it to keep the lump from sagging. When the lump is viscous, but not completely melted, pull the two rods apart rapidly, still in an aligned position, and spin the thread. Rarely are these threads consistent in thickness, being thicker where they join the rod. When cool, remove them from the rod by breaking or snapping them with the fingers. Never touch the residue of enamel remaining on the rod with the bare hands, for such portions are extremely sharp. Most of the residue can be removed by tapping the rod on a hard metal surface. Any final traces are best left on the rod, in order to attach them easily to the next lump.

ENAMEL FLAKES

Enamel for copper has a coefficient which is compatible with the metal; firing techniques include methods of placement in, and withdrawal from, a hot kiln. Unfortunately, this calculated rate of expansion and contraction does not coincide with that of glass, nor does the prescribed principle of rapid cooling indicate that these two materials should ever be combined, although both are chemically within the glass field. Certainly the coefficient of glass cannot be changed, nor can the necessary annealing process; and yet, the brilliance of enamel cannot be denied—as an accent, it has no equal.

In the section on lamination, we saw that techniques for background and design feature the use of enamels by permanently sealing them between two sheets of glass. When sifted on exposed glass surfaces, granular and chunk enamels tend to scale, leaving small crater-like depressions. This is the result of the two conflicting coefficients. On the other hand, enamel threads, which are processed from the raw chunk enamel, fuse perfectly to glass surfaces. One is forced to assume that a shrinkage takes place during the processing, and to conclude that the coefficient has been altered sufficiently to permit the use of this enamel form as a glass decorating material.

Based on this premise, experiments were conducted in my workshop which proved the theory to be sound. Granular enamels were sifted on 18-gauge sheet copper, and then enamel chunks were added, both in excessive amounts. The copper piece was then fired until the enamels became glossy, and the chunks completely flat. After cooling, the black fire scale (oxidation of copper, occurring each time it is

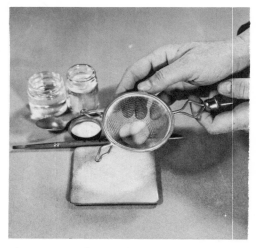

Fig. 180. Annealed sheet copper is sifted with opaque white enamel . . .

Fig. 181. . . . and transparent colored enamel is then added.

Fig. 182. Lumps of transparent enamels are placed with tweezers.

Fig. 183. After firing, the enameled copper is immersed in sodium bisulfate solution to remove firescale.

Fig. 184. The copper is twisted with pliers; sections of vari-colored enamel coating fall off.

Fig. 185. A fired bowl; enamel flakes on colorless glass.

heated) was removed from the underside of the metal by immersion in a 20% solution of sodium bisulphate.* The enameled piece of copper was left in the solution until the fire scale separated, after which it was removed with tongs and rinsed thoroughly with clear water. One side, or corner, of the enameled piece was twisted with heavy pliers, causing the enamel to fall off in flakes or chips. These flakes could then be affixed to a bare glass

* Dispensed under various trade names, sodium bisulphate can be obtained in nurseries, or nursery supply houses. For use in removing fire scale, it is usually mixed with five parts of water.

surface with oil, or scattered on luster or glass glaze for a confetti-like effect.

This simple process can be duplicated by using an enameling kiln, or even an ordinary electric hot plate, in which case the enameled copper is placed directly on the vitreous grids, and the unit covered with a Pyrex pie plate, to permit observation. Hot-plate firing takes a little longer than in an enclosed kiln, and removal of the hot Pyrex cover should be done with pliers, rather than a kitchen hotpad. The twisted copper can be flattened by pounding with a hammer, and may be subsequently re-enameled.

For the most part, opaque flakes

Fig. 186. Enamel flakes on a shell dish with glass glaze surface colorant.

are more effective when lumps and enamel ground coats are identical. Colored transparent flakes appear indistinct unless backed with an opaque, preferably white, to retain the original, selected transparent color.

The following combinations of colors may prove useful to those who are unfamiliar with enameling techniques:

White ground coat; additional sifting of:

1. *Transparent garnet;* chunks of transparent garnet, brown, turquoise, cobalt.
2. *Transparent turquoise;* chunks of transparent turquoise, garnet, emerald, cobalt.
3. *Transparent emerald;* chunks of emerald, turquoise, yellow, chartreuse, brown.
4. *Transparent cobalt;* chunks of turquoise, cobalt, emerald, garnet.

Iridescent flakes, resembling the nacre of blue tropical butterflies, require a somewhat different procedure. Burnish the copper with steel wool, or polish it with a copper cleaner, and then rinse it in clear water. Fire a normal sifting of soft flux, and remove the fire scale as above. Then oil the enamel coating (apply oil with the fingertip, rubbing gently), and gently transfer silver foil for enamels to the surface. This foil is delicate, and sections should be cut to size, if necessary, between tissue paper, sliding out the lower tissue as the foil is placed on the fluxed surface. Carefully smooth the foil by pressing from the center to the outer edges of the top tissue, then lift and discard the tissue. Transparent enamels, according to personal preference, are lightly sifted on the foil; transparent chunks may be added for concentrated color splashes. Then fire the unit of foil and enamel in the regular manner until the surface is glossy, and separate it from the copper by twisting. The thin undercoating of flux prevents the formation of fire scale beneath the silver foil, and forms a necessary bond between the metal foil and the glass surface. Any of the garnet transparent enamels cause the silver foil to appear golden instead of silver, which of course adds to the variety of planned color schemes.

When the flakes are refired, either on the surface, or laminated between two sheets of glass, the enamel coatings remelt, and tend to spread to some extent, beyond the foil. Since the enamel has been conditioned by the first firing, there is usually no release from the glass surface.

CERAMIC MATERIALS: FRITS, GLAZES, SUGGESTIONS FOR EXPERIMENTAL GLASS GLAZES

Ceramic Frits

Ceramic frits are fused combinations of raw materials used in glaze, or more rarely, clay body formulation. The primary advantage of these prepared compounds is that chemical changes of such raw ingredients have been effected in advance, ensuring a more predictable end result; unfritted materials can contain impurities, most of which are eliminated by the fritting process. Reactions of raw materials may depend on their geographical source, since many of the substances are minerals which are influenced by the presence of other metals in the earth. Certain soluble compounds are changed to insolubles by fritting, which eliminates many of the problems of glaze calculation. In some instances, the coefficient of the formula has been adjusted to correspond more accurately with that of the clay body upon which it is to be applied.

The difficulty in any reference to frits in general is that they may vary slightly with different brands. Although this is of little consequence in ceramic glazes having a higher melting point, these variables can be crucial when the frit is employed for glass decoration at a lower firing temperature. Analyses showing these differences have been published, but unless you have technical knowledge, selection is difficult. Recommendation of a specified frit may place an author in the unenviable position of showing favoritism toward some one manufacturer. For most of us, experimentation with our particular glass and firing conditions is imperative. Fortunately, most reliable firms co-operate generously in furnishing samples for individual evaluation. The obvious conclusion must be that those who are interested in experimentation must test the different frits and judge according to personal experience.

Opaque frits are generally the most satisfactory for glass decoration, the transparents tending to craze or to partially separate from the glass base. If you specify that the frits must become glossy at the lower firing tem-

peratures for glass, the firm representative or engineer will be better able to be of service. Although opacity is not truly typical of either the concept or the inherent function of glass, its judicious utilization is often desirable. From a structural standpoint, translucent or opaque frits, applied sparingly to windowpanes or panels, provide semiprivacy; as an element of design, they can furnish contrast to transparency, or strengthen ineffectual composition.

In appearance, fired ceramic frits seem closely related to enamels at lower firing temperatures, sometimes being slightly raised. This characteristic suggests obvious techniques of linear design, if mixing with water or media permits brushing or trailing from tubes or other tools. The consistency of such liquid or semiliquid forms determines the manner of application; thin mixtures usually spread on the glass, and thickened pastes may prove impossible to brush. Generally available only in white, frits to be prepared as liquids may be tinted quite simply by adding powdered overglaze to the dry frit before moistening, providing that both constituents are finely ground. Metallic oxides or coarse grinds of either frit or colorants require ball milling. Some satisfactory frits are available in crystal form, and these may be colored by brushing with overglaze or glass glaze. As the crystals are solid, colorants cannot penetrate, and therefore become tints rather than strong shades. During the melting there is usually some swirling of overglazes, resulting in a marbleized effect.

Ceramic Glazes

The use of ceramic glazes is also a matter for experimentation. Low melting glazes are often compatible with glass, especially those bearing special instructions regarding the possibility of running when applied heavily at the base of the ceramic piece. The craftsman who formulates his own glazes will, of course, have some idea of the type of glaze which can be expected to adhere to glass; purchasers of prepared glazes should enquire as to the nature of particular glazes. In any event, preliminary tests are essential. Fluxing components of the glaze must become at least viscous at glass-fusing heat, bonding to the glass base. Fusion must be accomplished by the ingredients of the glaze, or by other additives. One example is a very interesting combination of flux and glaze: an 06 (rather "stiff" semi-gloss) black glaze was applied sparingly to a glass blank. Dry flux was sifted lightly while the glaze was still damp. Post-firing revealed a glossy network resembling somewhat heavy veiling, such as is used for millinery. The idea of adding a material separately to lower the melting point of a ceramic glaze is still experimental, but I feel that the possibility of entirely new effects is limitless.

In conclusion, a word about the omission of specific formulas. Certainly the composition of many glazes is known. However, release of such information would be most unfair to manufacturers whose livelihood depends on processing and packaging, accompanied by innovations of the individual firms. It is therefore my policy to refrain from listing such formulas within these pages.

Transparent Glass Glazes

Aside from the wide variety of fluxes available by number from various manufacturers, I would strongly recommend the information given in *Ceramic Glazes*, by Cullen W. Parmalee, in his chapter on underglazes and overglazes. Suggested fluxes for overglazes can be adapted for use with glass, either as straight fluxes or as bases for transparent glass glazes, with overglazes used as colorants. None of the ingredients require a ball mill or any other professional equipment.

SUBSURFACE

The subsurface (underside) of the glass blank can be decorated within certain limitations. Fluxing agents, contained in most full coverage colorants, such as glass glazes, overglazes, and enamels, should not be used, as the subsurface is the area of the blank which rests upon the separator-coated shelf or mold. Although flux is a form of glass in the broadest sense, it is ground so finely that its melting point is far lower than that of the sheet glass in its thinnest formation. Consequently, coatings or even traces of highly fluxed colorants are apt to act as an adhesive between the blank and the separator.

There are, however, other media which contain a minimum of fusible agents, or none at all. Two of these may safely be applied to the subsurface: translucent ceramic underglazes, and metallic overglazes. The minimal flux content of the underglazes ap-

Fig. 187. Indentation of initial; formed by firing a glass blank over copper wire. The initial is copper wire in two sections, shown at the left. The bent plate has a pink luster surface.

parently is attracted to the glass blank rather than becoming fluid. Metallic overglazes, of course, are thin platings of metal which are rigid instead of fluid.

Application of both is described under "Lamination," and procedure does not deviate for subsurfaces. Placement of the proposed design, however, must be reversed if the blank is intended for bending, and is free-form in shape.

For subsurface use, linear or full coverage glass gold will require more drying time than that specified for surface decoration. When fired on the surface of the blank, metallic over-glaze is unharmed by the fumes engendered by its components, in a well-vented kiln; applied to the subsurface, and fired directly on a separator, the emanating fumes cannot escape, and usually discolor the glass. By prefiring the blank to 1000°F. (or cone 022), with the gold design uppermost, disfiguring fumes are driven off. After cooling, the blank may be reversed, and any colorant added to the surface, followed by a full glass firing.

Self-contracting gold, probably due to a lighter carrying vehicle, does not require preburning, and may be reversed and fired as soon as it dries.

Fig. 188. A nameplate, flat fired over the brass house letters shown. Chartreuse sheet cathedral glass was used. Glass gold was applied to indentations, followed by a second firing at a lower temperature.

SUBSURFACE TEXTURE

The subsurface of glass can be textured to serve as a patterning of the glass, or as a background for surface decorating.

Dry sifted whiting used as a separator provides a faint texturing of the glass, due to the repellent characteristics of the whiting. This tendency can be deliberately stressed, and the texturing deepened by riffling the whiting with a tool or comb, if such pronounced "modeling" of the glass does not interfere with surface design or sagging of a bent blank.

Flaked mica can be sifted on the separator before positioning the blank. Particles that make full contact with the glass will adhere during the firing. Although somewhat harsh to the touch, the roughness can be ground by rubbing with a carborundum stone. The mica creates a faint nonmetallic gleam when viewed through the thickness of the glass.

SUBSURFACE INDENTATION

Sheet glass assumes a sculptural quality, which is actually a planned distortion, when forced to bend or sag over an obstacle of any nature.

Fig. 189. An oriental cast iron dish (shown at the left) was used as a mold for the bent leaf dish at the right. The iron dish needs no venting since the sides curve below the highest points, permitting the gradual escape of air as the glass bends into the mold.

The obstacle, of course, must be deliberately contrived as part of the integral design, and must conform to the behavior pattern of the glass, i.e., it should not be undercut to such a point that the viscosity of the glass will prevent the release of the obstacle after firing, and it must always be coated with some sort of separator, for the same reason. It should also be so contrived that there will be enough free area of the kiln shelf or mold to provide the glass with a level post-fired shape.

Generally, simple linear designs, such as scrolls, initials, symbols, and primitive portrayals are more effective than intricate or elaborate motifs, as the thickness of the glass hampers the reproduction of sculptured detail.

There are several materials which are excellent for this technique:

Wire, in varying diameters (or gauges) produces fine lines.

Clay, because of structural characteristics, must be proportionately broad in area.

Metal can be either delicate or bold.

Any of these, placed upon the kiln shelf or flat planes of the mold, will cause sheet glass to follow the contours of such patterns.

Of the three classifications, wire that oxidizes when heated is the only material which need not be coated with a separator. Most alloys, being of unfamiliar composition, must be classified as possible attractors to glass. Clay will almost certainly adhere; though most of the clay separates for reasons of greater strength, the thinner stratum which remains is difficult to remove from the glass. These divergent materials will imprint or indent sheet glass satisfactorily, although each must be considered individually for best results.

Wire Indentation

Due to its malleability, pure copper wire is perhaps the easiest to shape. Insulated electrical wire, already annealed, is quite easily shaped, requiring only the removal of the insulation, which is readily accomplished with a sharp knife. Bare wire is often stiff, but becomes pliable when heated past 1000°F. Copper wire is obtainable in many diameters, referred to in measurement terminology as the gauge. Unlike the wire selected for lamination, no specific consideration for the

reaction of the glass is necessary; the wire, however, should be sufficiently heavy to imprint a distinct pattern. Single strength glass receives a clear impression from 14- and 16-gauge wire; double strength and $\frac{1}{8}''$ glass from 12-gauge.

Thickness of the glass determines the minimum space between the wires of any given design. The formation over wire must permit the glass to also contact the kiln shelf or flat area of a mold before rising over another section of wire, or control of the project, whether a panel or bent shape, cannot be maintained. For example: single-strength glass is $\frac{1}{16}''$ thick; descending to and ascending from a horizontal plane would occupy $\frac{1}{16}''$ each, so minimum spacing between wires can be estimated at $\frac{1}{8}''$. The design, of course, can be planned for wider spacing. For units which are complete in themselves, this same minimum spacing should be provided between the wire and the perimeter of the glass, as distortion of the glass on the extreme edge usually results in distortion of the entire concept of the design.

In order to indent level areas the completed wire design must rest flat upon the portion it is to occupy; even a slight lifting of the wire can cause a glass blank to shift during the firing from its original position. No section of wire should cross another, for the top wire will cause the glass to be elevated past the point of flexibility, putting undue strain on the blank.

Sketch the design on paper, and estimate the amount of wire by laying string on the sketch. The string can be straightened out and measured with a ruler, if needed for reference, or the wire can be measured directly from the string.

Use round-jaw and needle-nosed pliers to shape heavy wire; light-gauge wire is easily bent around brush handles, various sizes of doweling, right-angled wooden or metal forms, or merely with the bare fingers.

If the design is large, requiring many inches of wire, it should be revised into two or more sections; continuous lengths of wire tend to buckle when fired, whereas individual and separate units remain in place. During the shaping, place the wire design upon the sketch from time to time, to assure precision.

If the blank is to be bent on a mold, wire designs should occupy only those areas which are level, such as the rim or the bottom of the mold, for the sagging glass is repelled by an obstacle on sloping angles, and can fold back and/or over such mold cavities.

The wire design can be glued to the subsurface of the blank if the blank is to be fired flat. If bent, the blank is placed over the mold cavity, and the glue will burn out before sagging occurs, releasing the wire; therefore the wire should be placed on any level areas of the mold, allowing the blank to sag onto the design.

Oxidation of copper, also known as fire scale, occurs with each firing. This scale adheres to the glass, releasing the original wire, and may be retained as an accent to the indentation, or removed with a wire brush. The wire design may be used for subsequent firings, or reshaped to fit other areas.

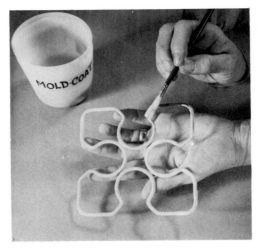

Fig. 190. A heavy brass trivet is coated with separator . . .

Fig. 191. . . . and placed on a kiln shelf. The glass panel is positioned on the wire.

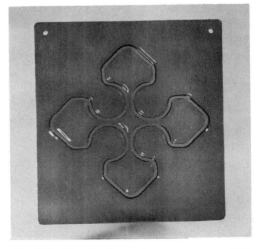

Fig. 192. The fired panel.   **103**

Fig. 193. A glass panel fired on a pierced clay tile.

Fig. 194. A glass panel fired on clay sculpture. (Both clay models are the author's originals.)

Fig. 195. Brass-wire indented disk—impression of candlestick base. The candle cup had been welded. A hole was drilled in fire brick to accommodate the inverted candle cup, allowing the flat underside of the unit to be used. The wire was coated with separator, then the glass was fired on the brick and wire unit.

Clay Indentation

Clay indentation, like wire indentation, consists of three-dimensional designs which are raised above the level of the flat areas of the kiln shelf or mold. Since clay is a plastic solid,

rather than a preformed product, it offers greater possibilities of design than does wire. It may be rolled into coils for linear design, modeled into low-relief patterns, cut into blocks, disks, free-form shapes, or letters and numerals. If the project is to be repeated, there is a definite advantage in making an entire clay form or mold, incorporating the desired design permanently. If the designs are to be utilized for different sizes and shapes, it is an easy matter to model and fire them separately, affixing or merely placing them on the kiln shelf or mold.

It is not the intent of this book to give clay instruction, except in the section on terra-cotta molds, which must necessarily be constructed to specifications consistent with the fusing of glass. Clay techniques have been most adequately covered, and there are many excellent books on this subject. It suffices to state that clay adjuncts must, of course, be fired, but

Fig. 196. Wire designs.

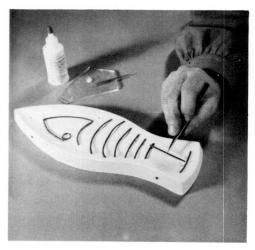

Fig. 197. Sections of copper wire are shaped and then positioned in a mold with tweezers. (Wires can be glued at the tips if they seem inclined to roll.)

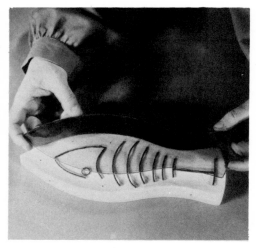

Fig. 198. The glass blank is then positioned on the mold . . . and fired.

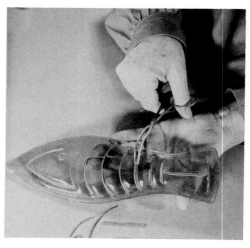

Fig. 199. The wires are removed from the sub-surface of the bent form.

Fig. 200. The indentation shows plainly through the upper glass surface.

should not be glazed. It is the manipulation of glass which is the primary theme of this book, and we will assume at this point that separate or integrated clay designs are available.

Clay, whether vitreous kiln shelf, firebrick, or soft earthenware bisque, requires a separator to prevent its adhering to the fused glass, and to assure subsequent re-use as a mold or model. Flat or concave surfaces may be coated with the separator by any of the three recommended methods: dry sifting, or by brushing, or spraying the separator in liquid form. Relief motifs, however, preclude the use of a sifted dry separator, for it is difficult to coat vertical planes; relief, whether clay or metal, should be sprayed or brushed. It is usually more feasible to affix or place the relief model on the shelf or mold, and coat the entire unit at one time. However, if one of the re-usable separators is used and the surface has already been protected, coat only the model, place it on the previously treated surface, and seal any gaps between the two by touching up with a small brush.

Metal Indentation

Although wire is most certainly a metal product, the fact that it can be shaped by hand differentiates it from the more restrictive techniques for metal in solid or sheet form. Unless you are also an experienced metal-worker, you probably lack the skill and equipment essential to produce such design as would adequately indent sheet glass, and must rely on pre-formed metal objects. Fortunately, excellent designs are available, although not in profusion because of the limitations imposed by alloys.

The manufacture of utilitarian or decorative objects from metals in the pure state is somewhat limited, because of factors of strength, corrosion, etc. Even gold, generally thought of as a pure metal, must be combined with copper, nickel, zinc, or cadmium, to provide strength. The combination of a pure metal with another modifying metal (or metals) results in what is termed an alloy. Of the metal objects suitable for glass indentation, only cast iron owes its prescribed form to the removal of impurities rather than the addition of other metals; even this statement should be qualified, for the degree of impurities remaining is an unknown factor.

Firing temperatures for the fusing of sheet glass range from 1300°F. for soft, flat-fired glass, to a maximum of 1600° for hardened varieties. Any extraneous additive must therefore be stable within this temperature range. Since the components of alloys differ, a brief résumé of the melting points of common ingredients seems desirable:

Brass is composed largely of copper, with a lesser amount of zinc; although the melting point of zinc is below the fusing point of sheet glass, the preponderance of copper raises the melting point of the alloy sufficiently to withstand the firing temperature of sheet glass.

Cast iron melts at approximately 2201°F., steel even higher. These two metals will not distort or soften when subjected to glass firing.

Bronze, an alloy of copper, tin, and zinc, melts well above the firing temperature of glass, due again to a major proportion of copper. Bronze reliefs, when obtainable in suitable design, are excellent for indentation.

Sheffield (a silver plating on copper), or any silver plating, for that matter, is deemed unsuitable for indentation because the thin plating may disintegrate under heat.

Those metals which have extremely low melting points, and which are not suitable for any metallic relief are aluminum, zinc, lead, and tin in excessive proportions. This established fact eliminates galvanized (zinc-coated) metals, pewter, tin, aluminum, and lead objects.*

* Data from *General Chemistry* (Young & Porter).

It is necessary to evaluate the selected object and test it by prefiring.

It is apparently not important to the usefulness of many fabricated items that the exact proportions of alloy ingredients be maintained. Within my own experience, the following observations have been recorded:

a. Of a set of eight matching Chinese brass drawer pulls, purchased at the same time and place, five emerged from the preliminary firing smooth and in the original state; three were extremely warped and badly encrusted. Removal of the encrustation showed that nearly half of the brass thickness had disintegrated.

b. Two Victorian cast-iron trivets, bearing the same trademark and identifying numerals, and cast from the same mold, behaved in a manner similar to the drawer pulls; one remained comparatively free from blemish, the other was markedly disfigured.

c. Two sections of perforated stainless steel, cut from the same sheet, reacted quite differently.

These diversified instances serve to stress the need for individual testing of any object to be used for indentation. Since metal objects should be prefired to burn out impurities which might rise to the surface, this preliminary processing also provides an opportunity to check stability; it is necessary to discard the project if disintegration is apparent.

Procedure

As was mentioned earlier, only copper forms a separator which could in any sense be considered adequate as a releasing agent. All metals react to heat, showing visible results after firing. These changes of the surface vary from the opalescent oxidation of stainless steel to the sometimes pitted appearance of cast iron, caused by attraction or amalgamation of impurities. It therefore seems practical to coat metal adjuncts (with the possible exception of copper wire) with a separator which will not disfigure the subsurface of the glass. (For types of separators, see "Separators," included in the section on Firing.

Metal objects are coated in much the same manner as clay models, but the separators adhere differently. Bisque absorbs moisture readily; metals, being impervious to some extent, depend upon evaporation to attain a set coating. A light film of separator, brushed or sprayed, and allowed to dry on the metal, will provide an absorbent base coat for heavier application. Be sure the metal is completely covered before firing.

Decorating

Although the sculptural quality of indentation often suffices as a decorating technique, particularly if the surface of the glass has been tinted, there are occasions when outlines of the pattern are indistinct, and the design weak. It is difficult, if not impossible, to predetermine the exact contact point of the fired glass, which precludes the possibility that the surface design may be co-ordinated on the glass blank with that of indentation. The indentation model, however, may be decorated after the separator has been applied; when the sagging glass

Fig. 201. An oriental cast iron disk is covered with separator . . .

Fig. 202. . . . and translucent black over-glaze is brushed on the raised design.

Fig. 203. A square of asbestos (also separator-coated) is then inserted in the opening; a turquoise stained glass blank is positioned on the iron disk.

Fig. 204. The fired blank. The underglaze has transferred to the glass. A hole was drilled near the edge for hanging.

comes in contact with the model, the decoration is transferred to the glass.

Translucent underglaze is probably the most satisfactory of the ceramic materials available, since it invariably contains flux, which assures cohesion. In addition, application of this medium is comparatively simple if the separator coating is approximately of the same consistency as the stiffened clay. Single, strong shades are suitable for bold or stark linear designs. Relatively broad, flat areas of the indentation model offer scope for two or more contrasting colors, the background light or neutral in tone, and any super-imposed design dark or brilliant as a contrast. As with other ceramic deco-

109

rating techniques, sharpness of detailed design depends largely upon allowing the background to dry first.

Liquid metallic overglazes (liquid glass gold, platinum, lusters, etc.) cannot be transferred in this manner. These materials must be applied to the indented glass, followed by a second firing.

Summary of Decorating Techniques

The foregoing pages have contained techniques for utilizing glass as a raw material to be converted into new forms; often with added colorants or other decorating devices. Although the actions and reactions of the glass and the various colorants have been discussed at length, a brief résumé seems desirable as an aid to the selection of the technique which will produce a desired result with a minimum of pretesting.

In general, the decorating of glass should be restricted to the materials that will adhere to the glass blank during fusion, and which will best carry out the original idea of the artist.

Specifics:

Texture: Laminated Non-Melting Materials

For an allover effect of a textured blank, carefully separate non-melting materials rather than applying them as a thick layer; this is most easily accomplished by lightly sifting or sprinkling them on the lower blank.

Mica Flakes. Uncalcined mica swells when fired between two sheets of glass, producing bubbles, sometimes known as "seeds." These may be combined with enamels for copper, ceramic frits, or with dry underglaze or overglaze;

their appearance is nearly always damaged by contact with moist materials.

Metals. Iron filings, carbides, and raw minerals such as biotite and vermiculite, while having no expansion under heat, often raise the upper blank because their compositions are incompressible. Iron can rust within the glass blanks if moistened; carbides sometimes assume the color of wet pigments such as glass glaze, underglaze, and overglaze.

Silica. Although silica is regarded as a constituent of glass, the melting or fusing point is generally so high that it is unchanged by the temperatures recommended for bent or flat-fired blanks. Sand or granite granules can take on coloration from moist pigments and often show iridescence after firing.

Texture: Laminated Fluid or Melting Materials

Crushed Glass. Colored glass crushings, for the most part, do not "jewel" or reach the three-dimensional balling cycle when laminated, because of the weight of the upper glass blank. They provide a minimum of depth effect and a maximum of pure color.

Liquid Glass Glaze. This liquid form of colored glass boils just before becoming fluid. The edges of the glass blanks have usually sealed before this stage, and consequently the trapped air makes bubbles. The form and location of these bubbles are generally unpredictable.

Texture: Surface

Crushed Glass. Both colored or colorless crushings react to heat individually on the surface of the glass

110

Fig. 205. A street light fixture. The original panels were replaced with colorless cathedral glass panels; superimposed bird shapes of yellow, chartreuse, and emerald stained glass were then glued to the surface. Small red beads were added for eyes. The foliage tracery, executed on the sub-surface of the panels with translucent ceramic underglaze, is shaded from gray to black. The panels were fired flat on a kiln shelf.

blank, each bit balling up into a jewel. The crushings usually adhere to other surface colorants; on undecorated glass, they must be cemented to the base glass with an adhesive. If the composition of the crushings is dissimilar to that of the base glass, the crushings must be extremely fine and well separated to avoid fracture.

Colorants for Glass

Enamels for Copper. These may be used for allover backgrounds, or

tamped with tools to form inlaid designs. They must be laminated to prevent possible scaling. Certain greens and blues are altered by the upper glass blank, and pretesting on small segments of the glass to be used is recommended.

Enamel Lumps. These have a tendency to lift from glass surfaces and must be laminated.

Enamel Threads. These threads may be fired on the surface or laminated. They may retain the raised appearance on the upper blank, but usually spread to some extent when laminated.

Fiberglass Threads. These tend to disappear on the surface, but retain their original thickness when lami-

Fig. 206. An individual panel of the fixture shown in Fig. 205, showing detailed composition.

111

nated. They may be colored with underglaze.

Translucent Ceramic Underglaze. This will adhere to glass because of the flux content of the formulation. Colors are unaffected by the glass blank or blanks, and should be selected as they appear in the unfired state. The fired surface is porous; projects requiring frequent washing should be laminated as a protective measure, although decorative wall or lamp panels are successful when this type of underglaze is used on the subsurface. Being non-fluid, underglazes are apt to show small fissures when the blank is bent into deep or abruptly vertical molds.

Overglaze. This is excellent for detailed or bold design work. It bonds well to glass because of the flux content and is usually more brilliant when fired on exposed glass surfaces, some color ranges becoming transparent.

Metallic Overglaze. Metallic overglazes for glass hold their metal appearance through the firing temperatures required for the fusion of glass. Deposits or platings of metal are rigid, and fissures occur when the glass is bent into deep molds. Contact with other unfired colorants should be avoided, and to avoid discoloration the inevitable fumes must be permitted to escape by ample venting of the kiln.

Glass Lusters. Lusters are more brilliant when applied to exposed glass surfaces, and generally have a pinkish or purplish cast when fired to the temperatures required for fused glass. The kiln must be well vented to permit the escape of fumes. Lusters are unsuitable for detailed design because of their transparency, and are usually regarded as allover colorants.

Glass Glaze. This is a liquid form of pure glass which bonds to glass surfaces. It is extremely fluid and is unsuitable for detailed design. Its main function is to give colorless commercial glass the appearance of more expensive color-impregnated glass.

Any of the decorating techniques can be adapted to any project whether small or large, the only differentiation being the brush or other tool employed; fine linear designs for jewelry require a fine brush, and the brush size increases with the size of the glass blank. Techniques can be combined within the limitations of individual procedures. Dry materials can be sifted on other dry materials or on liquid colorants. Mica flakes can be added to laminated dry colorants, either to provide bubbled texture or to accent a weak design with sparkle. Suggested combinations are:

For Single Blanks

Glass glaze; borders of sifted ceramic frit.

Glass glaze; metallic overglaze design on the subsurface.

Glass glaze; colored or colorless crushed glass as a jeweling agent.

Glass glaze; underglaze subsurface design.

Glass glaze; enamel flakes as a border or scattered on the entire surface.

Glass lusters; metallic overglaze design on the subsurface.

Glass lusters; enamel flakes as a border or scattered on the entire surface.

Metallic overglaze; etched in color with glass glaze.

Overglaze; outlined with metallic overglaze.

Overglaze; outlined with black underglaze lines on the subsurface. (This creates an illusion of depth.)

For Two Blanks (Lamination)

Lower Blank: Mica flakes ————— *Upper Blank:* Glass glaze

Lower Blank: Mica flakes ————— *Upper Blank:* Luster

Lower Blank: Underglaze ————— *Upper Blank:* Glass glaze

Lower Blank: Underglaze ————— *Upper Blank:* Metallic overglaze design

Lower Blank: Underglaze ————— *Upper Blank:* Overglaze accents

Lower Blank: Glass glaze, partial coverage ——*Upper Blank:* Metallic overglaze linear design

Lower Blank: Enamels ————— *Upper Blank:* Metallic overglaze linear

Lower Blank: Enamels ————— *Upper Blank:* Glass glaze, partial coverage

Lower Blank: Enamels, mica flakes ——— *Upper Blank:* Glass glaze or lusters as a border

Lower Blank: Silica (sand) ————— *Upper Blank:* Metallic overglaze linear

Lower Blank: Silica, light wash of—— *Upper Blank:* Metallic overglaze linear
glass glaze

For Three Blanks (Lamination)

Lower: Enamels ———— *Center:* Mica flakes ——— *Upper:* Undecorated

Lower: Enamels ———— *Center:* Enamel lumps ——*Upper:* Undecorated

Lower: Metallic over- —— *Center:* Enamels ———— *Upper:* Undecorated
glaze, full coverage

Lower: Ceramic frit ——— *Center:* Underglaze ——— *Upper:* Overglaze

Lower: Ceramic frit——— *Center:* Underglaze ——— *Upper:* Metallic overglaze, linear

Lower: Calcined mica —— *Center:* Enamels ———— *Upper:* Undecorated
flakes

Lower: Calcined mica —— *Center:* Enamels——— *Upper:* Metallic overglaze tracery
flakes

Wire indentation can be added to any of the above techniques or combination of techniques as a subsurface treatment, providing there is sufficient level area in a mold for the glass blank to form over the wire. For flat-fired panels, of course, there are no restrictions in the addition of wire indentation as an extra technique if the decorated surface is transparent or translucent enough to show the indentation. Prefired or self-forming jewels may be added for three-dimensional accents on the surface blank, if they do not detract from the original design.

As a last caution, the decorating of a glass blank should never obscure the qualities of the glass itself; sparkle, transparency, and fluid characteristics are easily lost in the enthusiasm of decorating. A very good test for clarity of design is complete visibility at a distance of three feet for small projects, at six to eight feet for medium to larger projects.

E. MISCELLANEOUS GLASS

Previous subject matter has dealt with colorless sheet glass and methods of cutting, decorating, and firing. Because of the comparatively close relationship of such commercial glass, it can be considered as a complete unit of reference. There are additional types of glass which lend themselves admirably to fusion, but which diverge in one or more aspects from basic procedures for handling ordinary glass.

STAINED GLASS

Within this category, stained glass, sometimes called cathedral glass because of its widespread use for church windows, more nearly approximates familiar techniques; it too is supplied in sheet form, thus enabling the craftsman to consider its possibilities as an art medium, and anticipate with confidence the ultimate result of a desired project.

Glass in sheet form must of necessity be cut to produce a planned shape, or a design involving sections. It is at this point that individual characteristics of the glass can become apparent, requiring special attention to, and possible deviation from, accepted procedures, to obtain maximum fired results. Reactions of specified substances to given circumstances or conditions become

115

Fig. 207. Drippings from ladles used in a stained glass factory. Bird; branch formations.

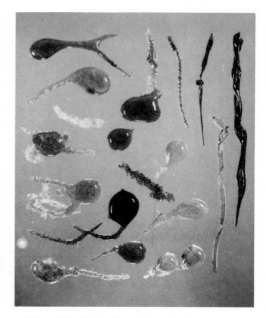

Fig. 208. Drippings from ladles used in a stained glass factory. Fish; seaweed formations.

predictable factors when they recur consistently; recognition and acceptance of variables are early steps toward the adaptation of stained glass for creative design.

Few who work with this material in the usual sense know the formulation of any brand or color, for it is quite unnecessary to be cognizant of chemical components to successfully execute a cathedral window. Stained glass is a chameleon material only in reheating. Firing to any degree can produce the unexpected; sometimes weird, often unpleasant, occasionally gratifying when routine firing schedules are followed. It becomes obvious that lacking knowledge of composition, the only means by which the craftsman can predict results is through the testing of each variety and color of stained glass selected. If exhaustive experimentation proves a specified glass to

be unresponsive, it is possible to switch to another brand. Three major factors influence the control of stained glass in its fullest sense. These factors are:

1. The resultant appearance of the fired glass;
2. The tendency of the viscous glass to attract chemicals in separators; and
3. The actual rate, degree, and atmospheric condition of the firing.

These factors all have a common denominator in fusion, for in each case departure from the predictable is definitely attributed to heat.

It is not unusual for stained glass to lose gloss at varying degrees of heat. Transparency, depth, and brilliance of color depend largely on surface gloss; hence it is of the utmost importance to retain the original appearance. Where test firings show frostiness or clouding tendencies, the addition of one of the fluxes for glass often performs like magic. No one flux can be recommended. There are countless fluxes, identified by numbers, the decoding of which is possible only to the manufacturer or packaging firm. Each, however, may contain some important substance which can have a definite bearing on a particular glass. Just as medical diagnosis and treatment can be complex, so may the discovery of the correct additive prove elusive. Fluxes for pinks and purples compounded with some form of gold are apt to conflict with cobalt-bearing pigments; lead fluxes, to which yellows and greens respond readily, can actually damage the surface of otherwise amenable types of glass, where no disfigurement should have been evident.

Lest you abandon the entire subject as being far too technical and entirely frustrating, without full knowledge of a specified glass, let me hasten to assure you that there are two ways out of the dilemma. First; rely completely on the manufacturer of fluxes (or the manufacturer's representative) to suggest, at least in a general manner, which fluxes will bring the best results within color categories. The manufacturer, although he may lack specific data on the type or brand of glass in question, does possess a working knowledge of which pigments will produce various color ranges, and he is usually most co-operative. Second; if the flux manufacturer is not readily available, you can, from a practical viewpoint, merely eliminate such types or brands of glass as seem unresponsive to the available fluxes. There are literally hundreds of varieties of fluxes from which to choose, and a satisfactory substitution for any desired color can be virtually assured with a minimum of preliminary firing tests.

Whatever the group of glass fluxes selected for evaluation, application should be very thin, as excessive amounts of flux deposited on glass create new strata of solid glass, not necessarily having the same coefficient as the basic structure. As discussed earlier (under Basic Procedures for Colorless Glass), a difference in coefficients usually results in partial or complete separation from the base.

Dry fluxes can be mixed with water, to a consistency that will permit scant coverage. Some fluxes are "fluffy" and absorb more water than others, so the exact amount of water must remain variable. For the most part, the minimum proportion is five parts water to one part flux. The flux coating must never be visibly opaque when wet, but should show as a translucent film after drying. No binders or hardeners which retard drying, or set up even a slight semblance of chemical action, should be added. Because of the fluidity of the flux when fired, vertical glass edges should not be coated unless the firing is to be extremely low in temperature.

All viscous glass must be separated from the kiln shelf or mold, to prevent sticking. Whiting (calcium carbonate, ceramic grade) is commonly used as a separator for colorless glass but the distinctive ingredients of stained glass may disfigure the subsurface when fired on whiting. This appears as a white encrustation, caused by a chemical combination which attracts the whiting to the glass, and this crust can be removed only by heavy grinding. For alternative suggestions, see detailed listing of possible separators, included in section on Firing . . .

Stained glass is brilliant in color because it is manufactured as a "soft," or low-fusing substance. Generally speaking, any stained glass will become viscous at approximately 50°F. lower than commercial colorless glass, although some colors require more or less heat than this arbitrary figure. Since there is no feasible way to harden sheet glass, you must accept the properties of this soft glass, changing your *modus operandi* to conform with the fusing point. In some respects, the lower temperature is a distinct advantage. For example, in the stained glass jeweling of a harder glass blank, it is not necessary to prefire rounded jewels, as jewel disks or blocks progress ideally to the balling stage of the glass cycle (see Basic Procedures for the complete glass cycle), while the harder glass merely attains a rounded edge.

These three differentials present the main obstacles in the successful fusion of stained glass, and though at times their control seems exasperatingly difficult, once surmounted by means of chemicals or rescheduling of the firing, they can be dismissed as deterrents. Responsibility should not be entirely relegated to the manufacturer of fluxes or kilns; you as a craftsman must be willing to run innumerable tests, if you are to have firsthand knowledge of the reactions of your materials, your kilns, and above all, your

own abilities. Bear in mind that only one problem should be considered at any one time; testing for two or more reactions precludes reliable results.

Compensating for all this effort, the inner fire and radiance of fused stained glass, obtainable with no other material, brings achievement and satisfaction of the highest degree in the ceramic field.

Possibilities of Stained Glass

Stained glass is a precious material. It is naturally more expensive than commercial glass, but its inherent qualities permit full use, from original sheet form to final by-product. Even with very careful planning, margins, corners, and some irregular sections must result from the cutting of the blanks. These can be set aside for jewelry, fragmentation, or fitted sections; in fact, they can be used in any basic technique as outlined for colorless glass. In addition, this scrap is invaluable for jeweling, whether the jewels are scheduled for colorless glass blanks, bisque or glazed clay shapes, fired individually for mosaic effects, or for open fragmentation of decorative suspensions (a difficult accomplishment with ordinary glass). Even the glass crumbs, usually swept from working surfaces as waste, can be meticulously accumulated if cutting or trimming operations are executed over clean paper or boxes. The movement cycle of glass subjected to heat is markedly apparent in stained glass firing, and even minute chips become individual glowing jewels no larger than the head of a pin. Used as borders on bare or decorated glass blanks,

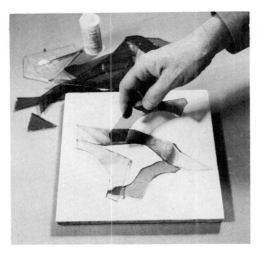

Fig. 209. Sections are cut or selected from scrap, and placed on a kiln shelf.

Fig. 210. Other fragments are glued over the joinings.

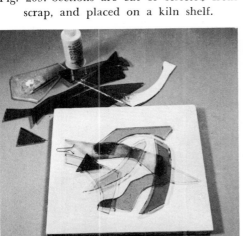

Fig. 211. A wire loop is glued to the top of one segment.

Fig. 212. An overlapping triangle is glued over the wire loop.

Fig. 213. The fired unit.

Fig. 214. Another suspension.

Fig. 215. "Pine Trees." Fragmentation of stained glass.

the crushings emphasize an otherwise shallow bent piece. Colors may be blended by scattering, much as enamels for copper are applied.

Unless the project calls for the use of metals which must be encased, such as screen for strength, or extensions of wire which will ultimately serve as a framework or stand, it is generally better to discard the idea of lamination, and work with the glass as originally selected. Intensification of cer-

tain colors by double thicknesses of glass often results in blatancy, and it is certain that darker colors cut down light transmission, so important to the beauty of glass projects.

Although there are hundreds of colors available in stained glass, there is always the possibility that for one reason or another (see Introduction to Stained Glass), you may not want to use an exact shade. The chroma can be altered by the application of glass

120

glazes as full coverage colorants. Being transparent liquid glass, they bond with stained glass without destroying its inherent qualities. They may also be partially applied to intensify shading, or to blend color change from one segment to another.

Metallic overglaze fires well on most stained glass. Being entirely opaque, it appears quite dark when illuminated. When it reflects light, however, the metallic gleam is brought into focus. It serves its purpose best when used in moving glass, as in windchimes; for heraldic design, or to provide a metallic background—if light is unimportant to the project—enriching the color of the glass above it.

Final by-products of stained glass to be used are the chips and crushings resulting from the severance of shapes or blanks, or from the rough shaping (with nippers) of square or rectangular blocks for jeweling. These can be applied to colorless glass blanks as colored texture, or added to decorated shapes prior to firing, as a border of texture, emphasis, or contrast of color. If a great quantity of crushings is required, segments or pieces of glass can be crushed by the procedures outlined on page 79.

There has been an interest on the part of structural planners, in attempting to adapt the brilliance and depth of stained glass by fusion to ordinary window glass, in irregular geometric design. Such combinations inevitably result in fracturing of the base glass, due to different coefficients. The desired effect can be accomplished easily by changing the base glass. To be sure, this will be somewhat more costly, but

in any case, custom windows would not be competitive with run-of-the-mill installations. There is colorless "stained" glass (uncolored glass from the same basic formulae as those used for colored batches), ranging from absolute transparency to heavily seeded texture. This glass, of course, has a close enough coefficient to allow the fusion of large segments without fracture. In addition, the elasticity of stained glass permits irregular weight distribution without rupture of the base blank or panel. By using this simple principle, it is possible to complete some projects which otherwise would be fractured in firing. The segments, like window glass or plate, may be glued in position. Use barely enough heat to dull the sharp edges of

Fig. 216. Fragmentation of stained glass shards, bent in a tree-shaped mold.

121

the superimposed segments. A higher temperature will start the "balling up," or jeweling cycle, which could end in the lifting of the base glass.

Cutting

The cutting of stained glass must sometimes diverge from established procedures for the severance of colorless commercial glass. To provide illusions of color depth, or to obscure outside vistas which would distract the viewer from the design of the stained glass window, irregular texture is often incorporated into the sheet on one or both surfaces. Bubbles, designated as "seeds," are sometimes introduced intentionally into the viscous glass batch as a texture variant. Both innovations weaken the structure of the glass to some extent, necessitating skill in cutting.

Instead of a continuous pressure in establishing the scored severance line, you may have to manipulate the cutter with a series of short strokes, stopping at each minute protuberance, irregularity, or crater-like burst bubble. Disregard of surface distortion dulls the cutting wheel, and the momentum of the wheel exerts undue pressure on areas where the panel is thin or suddenly unimpeded, causing it to split. This method is exactly opposite to that recommended for glass which is smooth and of uniform thickness; as a result, edges can be quite ragged until you achieve dexterity with the cutting tool. These rough edges can be ground with a hard carborundum stone, or an electrically driven rubber abrasive wheel, as outlined in basic cutting procedures. Where precise

cutting is not a factor, firing of soft stained glass heals uneven edges to a surprising degree.

Using a hard glass cutter and lighter pressure often minimizes any difficulty in scoring and separation of the desired shape.

Although this glass is considered soft as far as fusing temperatures are concerned, it is apt to be brittle in the physical handling, and both shards and edges are very sharp.

PREFORMED GLASS

A perfect circle is virtually impossible to cut with a hand glass cutter. While it is true that circle cutters are obtainable, they are an expensive investment if but few circular shapes are desired, and in some sections of the country they are difficult to locate.

Inexpensive cast plates are plentiful in most variety and chain drugstores. In addition to perfectly plain plates, numerous patterns are available. These patterns are formed by the modeling of the molds in which they are cast or pressed, and usually appear on the underside of the plates. For the most part, they are indented rather than protruding. The quality of the glass is indifferent. However, upon firing, a veritable miracle occurs. Easily bent, indicating a "soft" or low melting formulation, the surfaces of these plates assume qualities which are comparable with heavy crystal. Generally the plates are round, although a few semisquare ones have been noted. One type boasts pointed, petal-shaped edges (impossible to cut from sheet glass) and comes in three sizes. These are, indeed, a boon.

Fig. 217. Madonna panel. Partial lamination of stained glass. (Work of Jeanne Adams, Vashon, Wash.)

The plates, of course, must fit the molds for bending. A gently sloping mold without a flat rim may be used to bend a plate which has the same diameter as the mold, or is smaller, but the plate must never extend beyond the mold. The firing range of such plates is variable, some requiring temperatures equivalent to that of sheet glass, others slightly lower. Close observation of each new pattern is advisable, to make future results more predictable.

Sometimes indentations disappear in the firing, but the original designs can be retained through the use of a self-contracting liquid glass gold. Invert the plate and place it on a stilt or other elevating device, to allow minimum handling. After routine cleaning of the plate with alcohol solvent, apply the gold with a brush, in a light but complete coating. After drying for twelve hours, the gold application has contracted into self-patterns on smooth areas, sometimes in irregular tiny splotches, often forming into dots of assorted sizes. Draining into the plate indentations when first applied, the gold has little flat area in which to contract; consequently it hardens as solid coverage, and thus delineates the pattern. This form of gold need not be prefired to eliminate fumes. When dry, it can be placed directly on the mold separator without discoloring the gold or glass subsurface.

After the gold has been applied and is dry, reverse the plate and again clean the surface with alcohol solvent. A transparent colorant is almost mandatory, for the gleam of the gold would be obscured by opaque pigments. Glass glaze on the plate surfaces not only provides color, but is enriched by the gold flecks beneath. The usual methods of applying glass glaze are applicable to plates as well as to glass blanks.

The plates, of course, can be fired without the gold, in which case they may lose, or retain, the indented patterns. Either way, the fluid, thick richness of the glass itself is a delight to behold.

Initial experiments with preformed plates were based solely on the need to obtain circular shapes without the use of tools, and to have them available to groups such as those working with the very young or the handicapped, and recreational and educational institutions whose budgets did not permit purchase of specialized equipment.

Fig. 218. A heavy glass plate bent on a clay mold; the fluting formation resulted from ridges in the mold. The pattern on the bottom of the plate was retained by the application of self-contracting gold metallic overglaze prior to firing. Glass glaze provided surface coloring.

Fig. 219. A pre-formed heavy glass snack tray bent on a round clay mold. The illustration shows the original tray and fired bowl; surface colorant; glass glaze.

Fig. 220. A pre-formed glass cup. The illustration shows the original cup; the cup positioned on the clay mold. The fired cup (at the right) has bent into the fluted oval edge. The handle has closed and become an extension of one of the flute depressions of the mold.

Fig. 221. A thick bowl. The bottom is 2 inches thick, contrived by placing a glass flower frog in the bottom of the mold. The frog openings were colored with glass glaze. Bronze mineral flecks and mica flakes were placed between two glass plates; entire structure was fired in the mold.

Fig. 222. A side view of a heavy-bottom bowl, made by firing two free-form plates over a glass door knob. The unfired plates and knob are shown at the left. Enamels and gold glass crushings were laminated between the plates.

Fig. 223. A heavy bowl created by firing together two nested, thick, star-shaped ashtrays. Shape of the mold caused the points of the smaller ashtray to become rounded; the larger ashtray retained its original points to some extent. Surface coloring; glass glaze. Gold glass crushings were laminated between the two ashtrays.

Fig. 224. An extremely thick bowl made by firing together three glass ashtrays. The smaller ashtray is emerald green; the upper and the lower ashtrays are colorless. The unfired stack of ashtrays is shown at the right.

Fig. 225. A thick bowl, its extremely heavy bottom effected by placing a 1-inch thick sham tumbler bottom in a mold. Two glass plates were decorated and fired on top of the sham bottom. Laminated enamels, glass glaze and gold glass crushings were used as colorants.

Fig. 226. Assorted bottoms of tumblers and pitchers glued to a glass plate. The unit is shown on a clay mold.

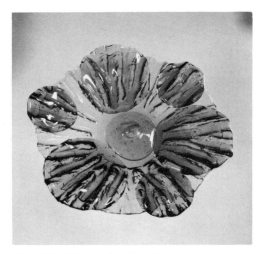

Fig. 227. The unit after firing.

Fig. 228. A Mexican tumbler. At right; two tumblers fired together.

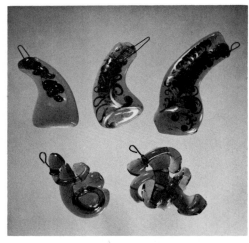

Fig. 229. Christmas ornaments—Mexican glass handles.

Fig. 230. Christmas ornaments contrived from Mexican wine glass shown at right.

Fig. 231. Assorted Christmas ornaments shown on a wire tree.

Gradually it became obvious that such glass possessed characteristics entirely different from commercial sheet glass. From the first, firings plainly indicated an early viscosity, always symptomatic of "soft" glass. Routine following of established techniques revealed an elasticity far exceeding that of the more familiar sheet glass. In accepting this special form it was necessary to re-classify glass suitable for use by the craftsman, and to examine existing differences.

Aside from the lower firing temperature, precast or blown objects assume a depth and quality not effected in the firing of sheet glass. In addition, extreme thickness fires without fracture and laminations fuse without visible signs of demarcation. Smaller and thicker items can be laminated between somewhat thinner plates, even those which are larger in diameter. These are the factors which make possible the execution of the thick European-type bowls by kiln firing. Procedure is illustrated in a series of photographs; see fig. 218-225 on pages 124-125.

Projects may be colored by using any of the materials listed for sheet glass, the techniques for specific decorating remaining unchanged.

Marine, aviation, and traffic-light lenses may be fired flat, or bent in a mold. Pyrex-type glass has a tendency to crystallize when fired; softer glass retains the original transparency. Apparently different glass batches vary, and conclusive predicability is impossible. Due to the current use of plastic for automobile and truck taillights, the older glass lenses are difficult to

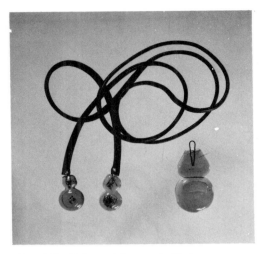

Fig. 232. Belt weights and Christmas ornament made from Mexican glass stoppers.

obtain, but are often quite satisfactory as a source of red glass when you can find them.

BOTTLE GLASS

Bottles assume qualities of sparkle, clarity, and depth after bending, that are assuredly not present in the original container form. While it is true that bottles collapse during the firing, thus creating lamination of any materials placed within, the resulting thickness of glass itself does not account for the remarkable feeling of depth; sheet glass of equal thickness

Fig. 233. Convex marine lens (left) became concave when fired on a square mold.

Fig. 234. The collapse of a bottle depends on its original shape. The upper form is the shape of the original bottle. (*Lower left*) The fired bottle. (*Lower right*) A larger bottle of the same shape.

may be laminated without gaining this characteristic. Evidently glass formulation and processing is responsible for the transformation.

Selection

The end (the bottom of the bottle when standing) is thicker, and always collapses toward the neck, whether bent in a mold or fired flat, creating a foldover of glass. The shape of the foldover, of course, depends on the shape and dimensions of the bottle. As a rule, square bottles are disappointing when bent, as the foldover usually bends into the entire mold cavity, filling it with glass to such an extent that there is little space for use as an ashtray or dish. Round bottles are apt to roll during the firing, since contact with the mold is a mere hairbreadth. The most predictable and satisfactory bottles are those of a width that exceeds the depth. (The word "depth" in this instance refers to the measure-

ment from front to back, rather than to the thickness of the glass.) Such bottles may be termed flasks, or slight ovals. Pint and half-pint bottles used by distilleries, medicine bottles, syrup and honey jugs, cosmetic bottles, are some of the shapes which lend themselves to bending. Whatever the shape, bottles should never extend beyond the mold or shelf.

Most liquor bottles have a thicker rim or collar, to strengthen the bottle for pressure-applied corks or caps. Although this thicker collar will bend easily, it is apt to snap off the bent piece at some time after firing, from sheer weight. To avoid this, sever the collar from the bottle prior to bending. Some bottles designed with flared necks are cast in such a manner that the collar is not an additional thickness, but merely follows the design of the mold, the glass shell being of equal or approximately equal thickness. Such collars need not be severed. If the neck opening is sufficiently wide to insert the smallest finger, the inside contour can easily be determined by touch.

The process of glass cutting requires pressure or tapping of a scored line on the reverse side, and it is obvious that there is insufficient room inside the neck of a bottle to tap an outside scored line. There are glass gauge cutters designed to score the inside of the neck at any predetermined depth up to 12". These cutters are arranged with a cutting wheel mounted on the end of a rod; a parallel rod with a wedge-shaped end slips over the outside of the bottle, helping to hold the cutting wheel in position. Scored lines

Fig. 235. Three bottles fired side by side on a clay mold. The interiors contained scattered bits of colored crushed glass and mica flakes.

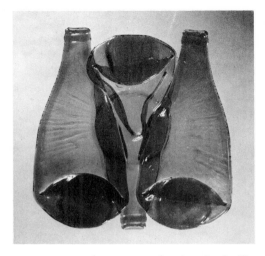

Fig. 236. Three green bottles fired side by side on a round clay mold. (Work of Mrs. Stanley Clutter, Inglewood, Calif.)

have more continuity if the bottle, rather than the gauge cutter, is turned. The outside of the bottle can then be tapped.

Gauge cutters, designed for neon and other glass tubing, are intended for parallel scoring, and unfortunately cannot establish contact with the bottle unless the interior diameter of the neck is the same below the collar as it is at the actual opening. They are useless for necks which flare or curve.

A scored line can be made by "sawing" a three-cornered file around the angle between the bottle and the collar. This scored line is on the outside of the bottle, and separation of the collar can be achieved by the use of small tile nippers or end wire cutters, placed at right angles to the filed scoring line at the neck opening. The pressure of the nipper or cutter should be light, to avoid breaking through the scored line. Depending on the weakness of the cast or blown bottle,

the breaking of the neck may be uneven. In many cases, this irregularity is inconsequential, as firing rounds rough edges nicely.

Fine bottle glass shards are extremely strong and almost invisible, so careful handling of broken pieces is mandatory for safety reasons. Thoroughly clean the bottle before

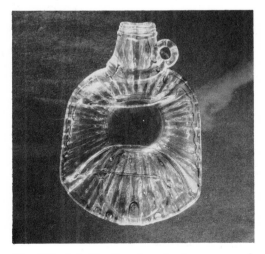

Fig. 237. A half-gallon jug, fired on a round clay mold. Surface coloring, glass glaze.

129

Fig. 238. Firing a hollow container creates a form of lamination. To ensure correct placement of the dry materials, the bottle is half filled with water and drained.

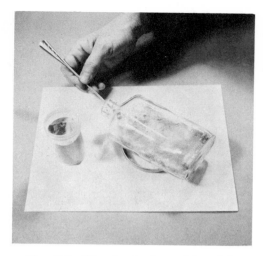

Fig. 239. The bottle is positioned horizontally. Transparent enamels are then conveyed to the interior with a long-handled spoon.

Fig. 240. Gold mica flakes are also inserted.

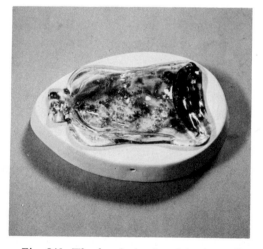

Fig. 241. The bottle is placed horizontally on the mold for firing. The illustration shows the collapsed bottle and the mold on which it was fired.

severing the collar, thereby minimizing the handling of sharp edges. Also, soak off the labels prior to removing the collar.

Inner Coloring

The collapse of a bottle fired horizontally is a form of lamination, and only those materials which have proved satisfactory in laminating sheet glass should be used. Another restriction is that the glass surface is inaccessible; brushwork is nearly impossible to execute on the inside of a bottle. Therefore, plan designs only for the top surface of the bent bottle.

Fig. 242. The bottle can be jeweled. Since the base will fold toward the neck during the firing, adequate space must be allowed. The estimated fold-over and the slope of the bottle are indicated with a graphite pencil.

Fig. 243. These jewels are approximately octagon-shaped. Strips of cathedral glass are severed into blocks, and the corners nipped off. The octagons are glued at spaced intervals.

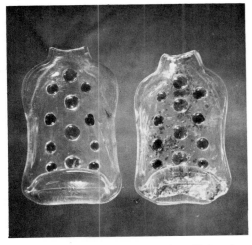

Fig. 244. Two jeweled bottles. Firing has rounded the octagon blocks into jewels. Mica flakes (right) add texture.

Placement of Dry Materials

It is difficult to sift coatings of dry materials through the necks of bottles by the usual methods, and the brushing of oil to secure the materials produces only partial coverage of the inner surface. Good results are obtained by filling the bottle with water, drain-

ing it completely, and immediately inserting the dry materials.

Place the bottle flat, preferably on an elevation of some sort for easy handling. (The open jar-lid rings used in canning foods are excellent for this, particularly for bottles which are slightly rounded.) Insert dry materials by using a very narrow spatula, or long-handled spoon, such as an aluminum beverage stirrer. For accurate placement, tap the spoon or spatula handle lightly, in order to dislodge the dry materials gradually. Two or more colors can thus be placed on adjoining areas, or blended together. Mica flakes may be scattered on the bare glass surface or on enamel or frit applications.

Introduce fiberglass threads into the bottle without attempting design placement—they form scrolls or patterns as they are forced into the bottle. If they are coated with underglaze, use no water in the bottle, since it would cause smears impossible to remove.

131

Small opaque glass beads, such as are used on Indian moccasins and belts, fire well as brilliant color accents. They may be added to dry material insertions, introduced as the only decoration, or strung on fiberglass threads. Any small beads can be inserted as decorating adjuncts, some transparent beads becoming opaque during the firing. Large beads may cause fracturing of the collapsed bottle.

Glass lusters are thin, and are best applied by filling the upright bottle so that at least the bottom is fully covered, then tilting and turning the bottle gradually until the entire inner surface has been covered. Draining the excess luster into another container may take considerable time. After draining, a bottle so lustered requires 24 to 48 hours' drying time, for although lusters dry quickly on exposed surfaces, little air can circulate through the narrow neck.

Surface Decorating

Remember that bottles generally are convex, and although they will bend into molds of adequate size, or fire flat on a kiln shelf, there is no way of predicting exactly *where* the collapsing bottle will form the perimeter of the fired object; the depth and shape of the mold cavity are as much a factor as the shape and thickness of the bottle. Extremely fluid colorants, buttons, beads, bits of stained glass, and enamel threads or flakes should never extend too far on a downward outer curve, as the fluid colorants tend to spread to an area which may become the subsurface of the fired piece. Superimposed glass and enamel

Fig. 245. A bottle suspension. Builder's metal lath and a wire loop were inserted in the bottle. Blocks of stained glass were glued to the bottle surface. The bottle was flat-fired on a kiln shelf.

threads or flakes usually separate from the bottle at an early temperature, regardless of the adhesive used to affix them. Apply these well within an area which will become the upper surface after firing.

Flat stained glass bits, enamel threads and flakes have an affinity for glass surfaces, and need only glue to hold them in place until bending occurs. Glass buttons generally are manufactured with tiny shanks, affording little area for balanced positioning on the bottle. Stained glass chunks are irregular in shape and present the same problem as the buttons. Glue burns out before 1000°F. is reached, while the bottle is still in its original

132

shape. Jeweling glass flux, applied to the underside of buttons and chunk glass, fuses to the bottle as the glue burns out, provided that such extra glass has not been positioned on a vertical slope. Apply the jeweling flux with a brush and allow it to dry; place the glue on the bottle by means of a toothpick. When the glue has lost its shine, press the glass chunks, buttons, or beads firmly on the glue, fluxed side down.

Balancing of superimposed glass is a delicate procedure, because strong adhesives can attach lightweight additions to vertical slopes; when the adhesive burns out, the glass bits fall off before viscosity is attained. An excellent way to pretest for possible gravitation is to place unglued glass segments on the bottle before glue is added; wherever the added glass will balance of its own accord should be the farthest point of attachment. Some flask-type bottles have one concave side, and if this depressed side is placed uppermost on the mold or kiln shelf, superimposed additions are subject to less shifting during the firing.

Metallic overglaze may extend over the bottle curve, since the viscous content of liquid metallics, which causes fumes, will have burned out before the bottle bends. However, the ultimate effect of linear design should be considered, for a continuous line crosses itself when the bottle bends and forms an edge. If design can be predicted, this result can become a planned technique.

Overglazes, being fluxed to some degree, should not be applied to any area of the bottle which will become the subsurface, for the mold separator will adhere to them, forming an unpleasant crust. Overglazes, generally mixed with an oil base, and metallic overglazes, should be dried overnight before firing.

Firing

When the bottle is completely decorated, again clean the underside with alcohol solvent to remove any fingerprints. If the bottle contains loose, dry colorants, it cannot, of course, be placed in an upright position. Hold it inside, or by the edges of the neck and the flat bottom of the bottle; these two spots will not be in contact with the separator, and any fingerprints will burn off.

The kiln should be fired very slowly, and with more venting than is required for sheet glass (1″ to 3″). Poised well above the mold or shelf, the bottle is vulnerable to sudden heat, fracturing easily in the initial stages of firing. If a pyrometer is used, adjust the door or lid to the usual venting of ½″ until 1000°F. Without a pyrometer, the opening can be gradually lessened, depending on the length of time the kiln usually takes to reach a cone 022 tipped. At 1000°F. (or cone 022) the kiln is closed for the rest of the firing cycle. Bottle glass usually takes a bit more heat to bend than sheet glass, the increased heat being required by thicker glass walls rather than the type of glass, for bottle glass is actually classed as "softer" than sheet glass. For bottle glass: 1525°F. in a kiln bending sheet glass at 1500°F., or an 014 cone flat in the usual ceramic kiln.

Fig. 246. The unfired bottle, and a flat footprint wire shape.

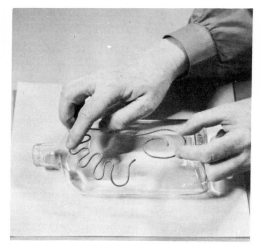

Fig. 247. The wire design is shaped to fit the bottle.

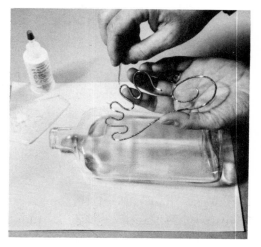

Fig. 248. Glue is applied to the inside of the shaped wire design . . .

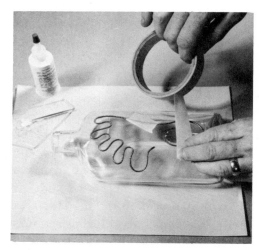

Fig. 249. . . . and attached to the bottle. To avoid loosening the wire, the design is also fastened to the bottle with masking tape. The bottle is then fired with the wire design on the underside.

The eventual subsurface of the bottle can be indented by means of copper wire, as outlined in the section on wire indentation, with one exception: since the area which will flatten cannot be accurately predetermined, the wire should be bent to the shape of the unfired bottle, and affixed with minute amounts of glue. It will then

indent the glass as desired, provided that the wire design does not extend to or past the outline of the unfired bottle.

Attenuated necks of long, slender bottles can be manipulated to form handles by placing a "bridge" under the neck prior to firing. These bridges can be carved from soft firebrick, or

134

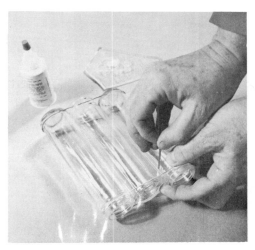

Fig. 250. Three narrow, cylindrical bottles are positioned with rubber bands and glued at points of contact. The openings of the bottles are alternated. The bottles are filled with water and drained.

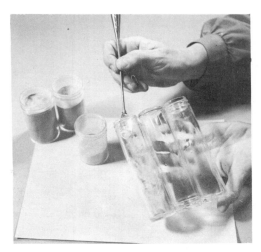

Fig. 251. Transparent red enamel is placed in the first bottle with a long-handled spoon.

Fig. 252. Transparent brown enamel is added to the third bottle.

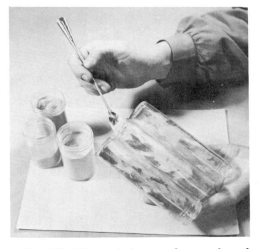

Fig. 253. The unit is turned around, and turquoise transparent enamel is added to the center bottle.

Fig. 254. Black enamel threads are inserted in all bottles by means of tweezers.

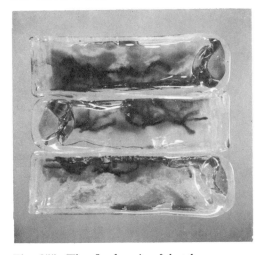

Fig. 255. The fired unit of bottles.

Fig. 256. A decorated disk made from the severed bottom of a brown half-gallon jug (shown at the left), decorated with a metallic overglaze motif. After firing flat, the disk was glued to a wire loop and the encasing glass section. The unit was then fired a second time.

modeled in moist asbestos (see Mold section, page 37). The asbestos bridge should be dried, and either asbestos or firebrick must receive a coating of separator. Bridges can be glued to the mold or shelf, or merely set in position without adhesive, if the bottle is perfectly balanced.

Two or more cylindrical bottles may be fired side by side, the separate bottles fusing together. Usually this procedure is reserved for bending, the mold serving to arrest any tendency of the round bottles to roll. The thicker edges caused by collapsing of the individual bottles generally form definite ridges when fused together, thus forming distinct divisions of the fired unit.

"Cream" type clear glass jars collapse into rondelles (flattened round disks), when fired in an upright position. Beads and small fragments of colored glass can be placed in these wide-mouthed jars, but materials which will not adhere to glass surfaces, such as enamels, should not be added, for the wide openings never quite close in collapsing. Colorants packaged in this type of container are adaptable for tinting the jars, since the jars are merely dried out when empty. This is a form of conservation, as it eliminates washing the jars or discarding them. The fired rondelles can serve as paperweights, or as a permanent reference for specific colors. A collection of rondelles suggests the possibility of "leading" or otherwise combining them to form framed window panels or panes.

A smaller bottle, with a correspondingly smaller neck, can be inserted in the opening of a larger bottle, if the escape of air contained in the bottles is provided for. Unless the diameter of the smaller bottle neck permits a clear

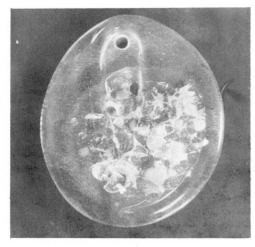

Fig. 257. Christmas ornament, made by firing a cold-cream type jar upright in the kiln. In collapsing, the neck of the jar folded in slightly, giving the rondelle an oval shape. A hole was drilled for suspension with nylon fishing line.

Fig. 258. Three cylindrical bottles fired on clay molds. The necks of the bottles become handles through firing over "bridges" of firebrick sections placed in the interior of the mold.

channel for venting, drill holes in both bottles to prevent the expanding air from exploding the bottles. The holes will not be apparent if they are drilled on the underside of the bottles. Illustrated is a cat suspension, contrived by careful selection of unfired bottle shapes. It is quite possible that "people" bottles can be created with further experimentation.

PREFIRED JEWELS

In the section on stained glass, procedures for the direct method of jeweling the glass blank were listed, this technique being dependent on the reactions to heat of two dissimilar types of glass, and possible only when soft glass is used for the jewels. Individual jewels, however, may be contrived from many kinds of colored glass, if the thermal variables are taken into consideration.

Although no accurate prediction is possible for specific brands, insulators and marbles are "harder" than bottle glass and bottle glass is harder than window or other structural glass. In turn, window glass is harder than art glass (cathedral, cast, or blown glass), and art glass is generally harder than beads or buttons. Thus it is obvious that no two categories will jewel when fired simultaneously, for if the harder glass compositions were to take precedence, the soft varieties would become liquid; inversely, jeweling temperatures for soft glass would not affect harder glass. The solution, of course, is equally obvious, being quite simply to fire such glasses as will attain the

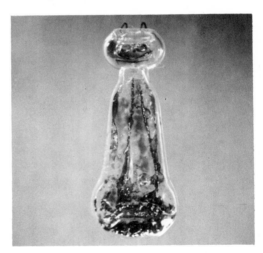

Fig. 259. A "cat" suspension. The body is a cologne bottle; the outlines of the feet were contrived by shaped wires inserted through the neck opening. The head is a purse-size perfume bottle. Wire ears were shaped and glued to the underside of the bottle with an encasing segment of glass. The neck of the smaller bottle was inserted into the cologne bottle opening before firing. The maroon coloring was achieved by following the technique of enamel placement. The unit was flat-fired on a kiln shelf. Its wire ears permit suspension by fishing line.

137

Fig. 260. Bottles are broken; small segments are severed from the larger sections with nippers. The segments are positioned on a separator-coated shelf with tweezers.

Fig. 261. The fired bottle glass jewels.

Fig. 262. Jewels may be large or small . . .

Fig. 263. . . . or fully rounded, or flat for mosaic use. Flat, angular jewels are achieved by less heat, as shown at the top of the shelf.

Fig. 264. Jewels made from a preserving jar, pale blue in color.

"balling" or jeweling stage during any one firing.

The structure of jewels is vastly different from expanses of sheet glass, in that each jewel is individual, and free to evolve without surface tension, expanding when heated and contracting as it cools, unhampered by attachment or the thermal shock of unequal surface temperatures. Jewels can

Fig. 265. Small vials are partially filled with alternating layers of enamel . . .

Fig. 266. . . . black enamel threads added . . .

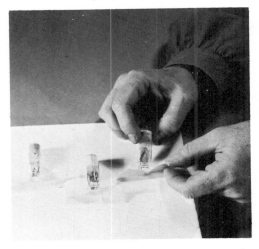

Fig. 267. . . . and the openings of the vials are sealed with masking tape. They are then positioned on a separator-covered shelf. The extended tape holds the vials in place. The vials are then flat fired.

Fig. 268. The fired vials are severed with nippers, then refired.

therefore be withdrawn from a hot kiln without fracturing. While this advantage is impractical for the ceramic or high-temperature kiln, the craftsman who has enameling equipment can produce large quantities of jewels in a short time. In addition, he benefits from being able to observe visually, without danger, the exact development of the jewels.

Fig. 269. The fired jewels are multi-colored.

Fig. 270. Stained glass jewels, fired on sheet mica (shown at the left).

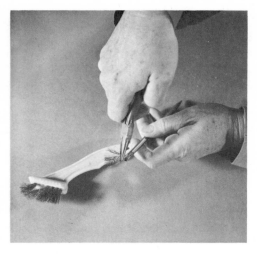

Fig. 271. A miniature wire brush is contrived by inserting one tuft of wire into the ferrule of a discarded decorating brush.

Fig. 272. Excess mica is removed from the back of the jewels. (*Note:* mica prevents fusion of the jewel to glass for subsequent projects.) The finished mica-fired jewels show a pronounced iridescence.

Fig. 273. Shards of various colored stained glass can be glued together to produce multi-colored jewels.

Depending on their ultimate use, the jewels may actually be flat segments with rounded edges, for subsequent mosaic techniques, or fully rounded three-dimensional cabochons. Either stage is determined by the termination of the firing schedule at the discretion of the craftsman.

Procedure

Place broken, irregular, or evenly cut pieces of glass on firebrick or kiln shelves which have been coated with any recommended separator as listed under "Firing." The glass pieces should be placed approximately ¼" from the shelf or firebrick edges, and

140

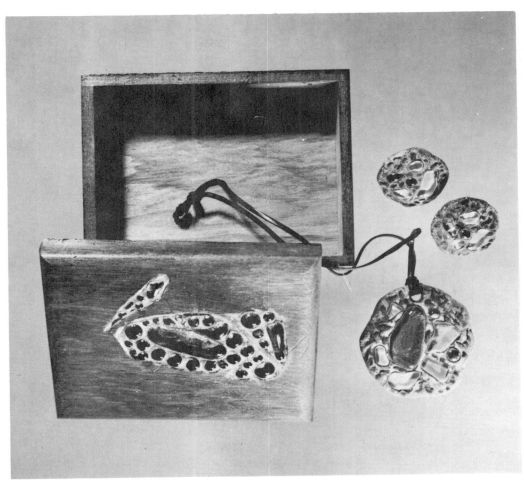

Fig. 274. A jeweled wooden box lid; earrings and pendant.

from each other. Use tweezers for easier placement. Position larger or thicker pieces to receive maximum heat; smaller or thinner segments should be placed proportionately away from the elements. In this manner, all sizes will jewel at approximately the same time. Since the jewels can be withdrawn from the hot kiln, additional "loads" can be prepared in advance, or while the kiln is in operation. For convenient removal, elevate the shelf or firebrick on kiln posts laid horizontally on the floor of the kiln, to permit an enameling fork, spatula,

or flattened coal shovel to be inserted underneath.

To obtain iridescence, fire the glass bits on sheet mica. The mica should be separated from its main portion in as thin a layer as possible, for mica swells during the firing, and thickness lifts the subsurface of the glass in the swelling process. If the mica-fired jewel is to be refired on glass, any excess particles of mica should be completely removed with a stiff wire brush, for the characteristic of separation would prevent the fusing of the jewel to the glass blank.

141

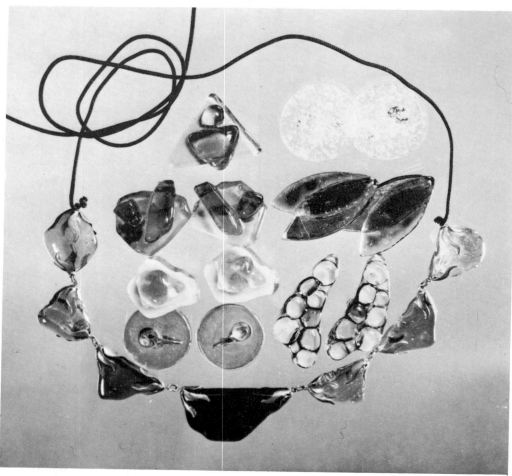

Fig. 275. Jewelry—assorted techniques.

If any particular glass loses its gloss repeatedly, this may be remedied by applying a thin film of glass flux prior to firing.

Colors as well as types of jewels can be segregated and stored separately for instant selection as needed.

CHUNK FLINT GLASS

One of the forms of glass recently brought to my attention is colorless flint glass in thick chunks, varying from approximately the size of kernels of corn to ten-pound slabs. This glass sparkles with an inner radiance, and nearly every piece shows iridescence, which unfortunately disappears during any reheating or firing. It has an extremely low melting point, making possible the construction of thick, massive bowls resembling quartz. One of its visible characteristics is a definite ring enclosing a somewhat higher center dome, called "onion peel." These formations may be large or small and some of the original larger patterns are discernible as partial radiating circles on the smaller pieces. Sensitive even to body heat, chunks may be easily severed with tile nippers after holding in the hand for a few minutes. The individual segments fuse about 100°F. earlier than the temperature required for the bending of window glass, and approximately 50°F. less than the fusing point of stained (cathedral) glass. Its many facets provide light refraction, thus creating extraordinary brilliance and depth. At the suggested firing temperatures, any sharp edges are merely blunted, while original conformations are retained.

Since the chunks are positioned prior to firing, there will not be the excessive strain present when sheet glass is bent into a mold, and it is therefore quite feasible to use a piece of ceramic bisque rather than a clay mold, for the shaping of the bowl. A mold, of course, can be used if you prefer. In either case, the clay form must be protected from the viscous glass by a separator. Since dry separators, usually sifted on the mold, are easily dislodged by the placement of the chunks, a liquid separator, which dries to a solid coating, is imperative.

Procedure

After spraying or brushing the separator on the bisque or clay mold and allowing it to dry, place the chunks in the form, starting at the center, or bottom, and radiating outward and upward as the project progresses. The chunks need not fit precisely, although they should be selected for similarity of outlines. Matching thickness is not a factor, for this type of glass bonds perfectly; low and high points actually add to the general brilliance. Each chunk, however, should have maximum contact with adjoining sections.

In lining the level bottom of the bisque or mold, gluing is unnecessary. When the contour of the clay shell starts to rise, a minute amount of glue, applied only to a few points, will hold the pieces in place. The chunks should not extend beyond the edges of the clay form, and it is at this point that unsuitable chunks may be cut to make them the correct height. Unlike mosaic techniques, the finished bowl does not require a continuous outer edge; irregular outlines add to the general appearance.

Set the bowl aside to dry overnight, and then it may be tinted. Complete transparency is desirable, to retain the inherent qualities of this flint glass, and liquid glass glazes provide a wide range of colors to match, accent, or blend with almost any color scheme. Apply the liquid glass glaze sparingly with a medium-sized brush, working from the low to the highest points of each facet. Color only the upper, protruding facets, eliminating the possibility of any surplus seeping through joinings of the chunks and onto the mold or bisque. One or more colors may be employed; the bowl illustrated is predominantly turquoise, with a few random chunks colored with chartreuse and pale emerald green.

Observation of the thermal reaction of this glass, and the obvious advantage of early fusion with minimum contact, suggest future projects impossible to achieve with sheet glass, especially within hitherto restricted areas where solid glass structure has been specified. It would seem to be entirely possible that irregular three-dimensional forms could be con-

Fig. 276. Various sizes of chunk flint glass.

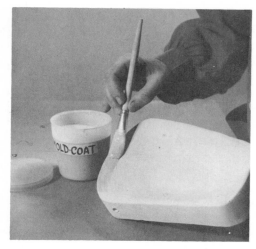

Fig. 277. Separator is brushed on a mold.

Fig. 278. Chunks are then placed in the mold, starting at the center . . .

Fig. 279. . . . and finishing at the edge of the bowl. The upper chunks may require the addition of glue.

structed without retaining walls of any kind, and that predetermined sculpture could be effected within the confines of simple molds. Whether this glass could be melted successfully at a higher firing temperature and within molds, as a kiln-casting technique, is a matter of conjecture at this time.

NOVELTY GLASS

So-called novelty glass seems to be classified as to its ultimate use rather than as a type of glass. Important only as a means of decoration, or for the introduction of miniature examples of glass-blowing artistry, the use of such glass is hardly a technique in itself. It must be imported and cannot be reliably duplicated, for European and Oriental manufacturers have a way of diverging from their original formulae. Haphazard as this system is, use of the glass often provides exciting finishing touches for unusual projects.

144

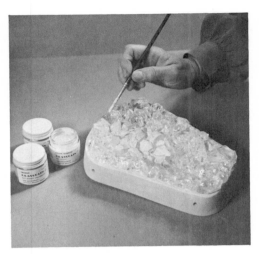

Fig. 280. Glass glaze is applied to the upper exposed facets of the chunks.

Fig. 281. The fired bowl.

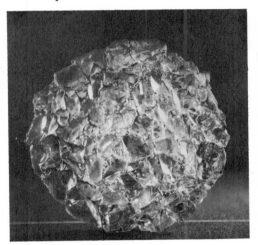

Fig. 282. A round bowl of chunk flint.

Fig. 283. A paperweight. Small chunks were fired within clay rings.

Inexpensive glass bracelets from India range from vivid opaque composition to intricately entwined threads of glass. Set in place as circles, or broken into sections, these may be superimposed on glass blanks as individual imagination dictates. The butterfly shown in the colored illustration insert indicates how wing structure and design can be suggested.

The majority of beads come from Italy. Too varied for accurate description, they may be transparent or opaque, flecked with gold or copper as in the larger trays or bowls, minutely patterned with geometric or floral designs, or striped in multicolors. The beads can be crushed, or fired whole, either on the surface or laminated between two blanks. Since they spread as they melt, the floral and geometric designs enlarge into more important designs, and are especially magnified when laminated.

145

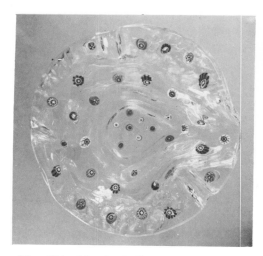

Fig. 284. Mosaic Italian cane segments laminated between two thick glass plates.

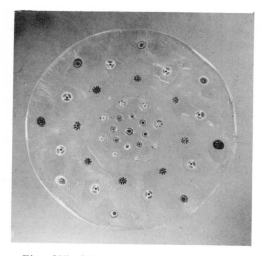

Fig. 285. Mosaic Italian cane segments laminated between medium-thick glass plates.

Buttons manufactured in West Germany and the Orient are particularly useful when used for the eyes of fish and animals, where diameters depend on uniform glass content. The pierced shanks provide accurate channels for the placement of fine wire loops or extensions.

With few exceptions, the novelty glass tested fired well with either commercial or cathedral glass.

GOLD GLASS CRUSHINGS

The extensive importation of heavy glass objects which appear to contain deeply imbedded flecks of metallic gold has created a considerable interest in this effect, and many questions have been raised concerning a possible material or technique. Since the metallic flecking of the imported merchandise is incorporated in the molten glass prior to blowing or casting, orthodox manufacturing procedures are out of the question for the craftsman.

First of all, it is a foregone conclu-

sion that any material used must be laminated to achieve the illusion of great depth. Lamination produces some weird and often undesirable results; colors can change, designs are sometimes distorted; certain metals, stable when fired in direct contact with kiln atmosphere, are apt to disintegrate or liquefy when encased in glass. Experimentation proved that even pure gold appeared dull, or became discolored when laminated. The calcined form of lepidolite (or mica), which produced a metallic gold gleam when laminated between double- or single-strength glass, was indistinct when thicker sheet glass was employed. Glass gold, dried and fired without the supporting structure of glass, remained dark in subsequent firings. It therefore became apparent that if glass gold, the most promising of the metallic compounds, was to be used, it had to be fired first on glass itself. However, even the thinnest of picture glass resulted in a flowing, to some degree, of the glass base for the gold. The final solution emerged when other types of glass were considered. Light and flash bulbs were tested, and were found either to melt too early, or to acquire translucence. Thin ampules, designed to contain liquid drugs or other medicines, were refractory, firing crystalline, and thus nullifying the metal gleam. Finally, Christmas ornaments provided the perfect vehicle, supplying the minimum amount of glass in relation to the maximum amount of gold plating. Even within this selected field, however, evaluations were necessary, for it was found that the melting points of ornaments differed, the softer glass diffusing the gold instead of becoming metallic pinpoints of reflection.

F. GLASS AND CLAY

GRILLES

In contemporary architecture, there is a definite trend toward open grille work, ranging from cement blocks to wrought iron. Interiors share this popularity, as evidenced by the demand for room dividers and screens. How fortunate, then, is the craftsman who can combine two familiar materials which meet the requirements for such functional use.

Clay fired to maturity is very nearly indestructible as far as time is concerned. It would be folly, however, to conclude from this simple statement that an entire modern building could be constructed from one mass of clay;

like other structural materials, clay has limitations imposed by the characteristics of its components. Exceedingly strong in smaller portions, clay disproportionately loses this advantage in excessive amounts, unless supplemented by reinforcement.

Glass in any form is easily damaged, due to its brittle nature. Redeeming factors are the transmission of light, and imperviousness to moisture.

Consideration of the best qualities of these dissimilar materials narrows the field of possible projects somewhat, but also clarifies the extent to which they can be safely combined. Actually, the limitations of either can be offset by the positive traits of the other. Thus, a frame or grille of clay not only confines the glass, but strengthens and protects it. The glass, in return, permits the use of clay in constructing windows, light fixtures, and dividers. Glass, of course, can be framed with metal or cement; the primary benefit to be derived from the fusion of glass to clay is that the completed unit is permanent without further engineering.

Glass as a material reacts to heat in an undeviating cycle, which has been described in previous techniques. When used in combination with clay, additional characteristics must be evaluated. Fine crushings are really separate particles of glass, becoming a uniform mass only when subjected to sufficient heat. Each tiny bit reacts individually, but with a group tendency of attachment. Clay, being of a different nature, must be provided with a fusible coating in order to attract the melting glass. Ceramic glazes that are compatible with the clay require more heat than will support the original glass structure, resulting in loss of brilliance, transparency, color, and texture. In any case, the glass always produces a fine network of fractures which indicate weakness.

The solution, if the glass is to be of primary importance, lies in reducing the fusing point of the ceramic glaze, rather than sacrificing the qualities of the glass. It is seldom possible to adjust a ceramic glaze to this extent without having it craze or shiver on the ceramic body, for equal or compatible coefficients of the two require a higher temperature. Experiments have shown, however, that certain glass glazes, used sparingly on the clay body and acting as a sealing coat rather than as a thick covering, could be substituted for ceramic glazes. At the lower firing temperatures, they proved entirely satisfactory in attracting the glass and adhering to the clay without crazing.

For this technique, the clay framework should feature flat surfaces and vertical walled openings, rather than elaborate sculpture or modeling of the clay, since it is difficult to control finely crushed glass on different levels. Pierced tiles with adequate openings can be constructed by following any of the well-known slab methods, or castings from ceramic molds may be procured, the latter being of particular value where architectural specifications require exact measurements.

The tiles must be bisque-fired to the maturity of the clay used and, since clay bodies vary in different localities and often with different brands, the maturing temperature should be ascertained from the supplier of the modeling clay or castings. If the exposed clay surfaces are to be glazed, such glazing and subsequent firing should be executed prior to the addition of the glass. True terra cotta or stoneware tiles will not require glazing if natural earth colors are suitable for the final product. Earthenware bodies should be glazed for protection if the tiles are to be part of any exterior structure.

Hollow-cast tiles may be prepared for future multiple-mounting in the following manner: drill holes in the edges of the tile, near the corners, using a clean, sharp $\frac{5}{16}''$ or $\frac{3}{8}''$ drill (either a twist drill or the flat-bladed type with a point at the center). It is better to drill the holes while the tiles are at the leather-hard stage, to avoid cracking the corners. A right-angle template of thin metal is recommended, with a small hole in each arm of the template for locating the center of the holes to be drilled in the tiles. The template holes should be at equal distances from the angle, and placed so that rods will be able to pass freely through the center of the outside tile border. Drill two holes at each corner (eight holes per tile), so that the tiles may be turned in any direction, or rearranged at a later time. If the final arrangement of the tiles is known definitely in advance, the holes in the left and right edges may be omitted, and only four holes drilled (two top and two bottom). When the drilling is finished, hold the tile up to the light, and remove any interior bits of clay which might obstruct the mounting rods.

After the preliminary mechanics of the clay framework have been completed, coat the inner walls of the tile openings with the glass glaze mentioned earlier. The bisqued clay, particularly if it is the more porous earthenware, will have a tendency to "grab," or absorb, the liquid content of the glass glaze rapidly. This difficulty can be overcome by thinning the glass glaze with water, dampening the bisque, or by merely dipping the brush in water before each application of the glass glaze. Depending on the type of glass glaze used, one thick, or two thin coatings are sufficient to seal

and color the clay. Any traces of the glaze on the underside of the tile should be removed.

Coat the kiln shelf on which the glass-filled tile is to be fired with a liquid separator; dry sifted separators are not desirable, as they are apt to work into the fine particles of glass, interfering with complete fusion.

After thorough drying of the tile and kiln shelf, strap the tile to the shelf with masking tape, or if the separator is of the type that will not permit adherence of the masking tape, place a plastic bag on the shelf, and glue the tile to the plastic. (Glues recommended for other glass techniques, plastic bags, and masking tape burn out during the glass firing.)

Slowly fill the tile openings with the finely crushed glass to the upper level of the tile. Demitasse spoons are excellent for filling small openings. Tamping occasionally with a wire, where the walls of the openings join the shelf, may be necessary to insure that the openings are completely filled.

The tile and glass unit may then be conveyed to the kiln with minimum dislodgement of the crushed glass.

If colorless commercial glass crushings are used, they may be tinted by dripping one or more colored glass glazes onto the filled tile openings, with a medicine dropper or brush.

Stained glass crushings need no added colorant, and shades may be blended by alternating and overlapping colors as the openings are filled.

For specific firing instructions for various types of glass, see the section on the cycle of glass subjected to heat (page 23).

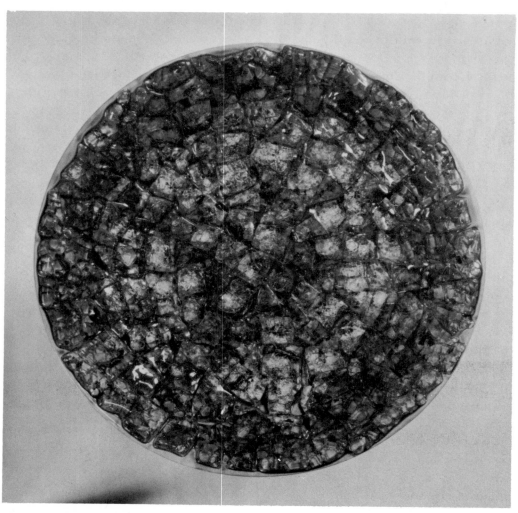

Fig. 286. Glass shards on ceramic bisque.

Pierced tiles may be used singly or in groups; positioned in windows, they become decorative transparencies. Or they may be cemented in niches or garden walls, placed beneath rows of flowerpots, etc. Interesting patterns may be worked out by alternate turning of individual tiles in a group.

Individual tiles, or single rows of tiles, may be framed with grooved metal or wooden materials, if the channeling matches the thickness of the tile. Units of four or more tiles make excellent room dividers or Shoji

(portable) screens. Here is one method of multiple mounting. Use a simple wooden frame to hold the tiles firmly together; pass $\frac{1}{4}''$ metal rods through holes in the edges of the tiles, and into holes drilled in the top and bottom of the frame. Vertical rods are preferable to horizontal, to avoid strain and sagging at the center of the unit. For small groups of tiles, $\frac{1}{4}''$ wooden doweling may be used in place of rods. The most accurate mounting may be achieved by completing and firing the tiles, placing them on a flat surface in the desired arrangement, passing the rods through them, and then marking the frame for drilling to receive the ends of the rods.

Short sections of dowel can be substituted for continuous rods if the tiles are of solid clay, and have been drilled to receive the dowel.

Ultimate installation of a multiple unit should be planned in advance; careful measuring and drilling will be rewarded with a neat, firm tile unit.

SHARDS ON BISQUE

The cutting of glass blanks inevitably results in an accumulation of scrap glass, a good portion of which consists of margins and corner sections removed from circle or free-form shapes. While much of the scrap can be used for small projects such as jewelry, wind-chimes, and Christmas ornaments, there will always be more than the average craftsman will want to allot for such specialized items. The excess need not be consigned to the trash barrel, fortunately, for the glass can be combined with clay to create a technique which cannot be classified as belonging solely to either material.

Procedure consists of lining a clay bowl with small sections of glass, which can be of the same thickness and brand, or varying in type, for in this project, each shard will fire as an individual unit without a stress reaction from an adjoining segment.

A bisqued shape, either hand modeled or cast, is selected as the base to which the scrap glass will be added. Inner walls should slope gradually and be without convolutions, to facilitate arrangement of the glass.

The scrap glass, generally irregular,

can be prepared in advance, and selection of the individual shards made from an assortment at the gluing stage, or desired shapes may be severed from the scrap as needed. The shards should be of fairly uniform size, although precise fitting is unnecessary. In fact, occasional small areas of exposed bisque, where the segments join, is desirable, as they afford a greater flexibility for the glass to expand in firing. Shards can be severed with tile nippers or end-wire cutters.

Glue the shards to the bisque with any of the adhesives which have proved satisfactory for fired glass. Starting at the center of the bisque shape with the first shard permits encircling segments to radiate fairly evenly, if the size of such segments is proportionate. When the bisque walls start to slope upwards, this alignment is easier to follow than if the glass is placed at random, for the gradual filling of one large area is simpler than trying to fit shards into many decreasing spaces. Small amounts of glue, applied with a toothpick at one or two places on the underside of the glass, will suffice to position the shards firmly. Each shard should contact adjoining ones in at least two places, particularly on the sloping walls, where such contacts serve to minimize possible shifting of the shard. Continue gluing the glass until the entire interior of the bisque shape has been covered. Final placement at the edges of the bisque form will require more precision, for no portion of glass should extend beyond the limits of the bisque. Allow ample drying time, usually 24 hours, before applying any liquid colorants.

153

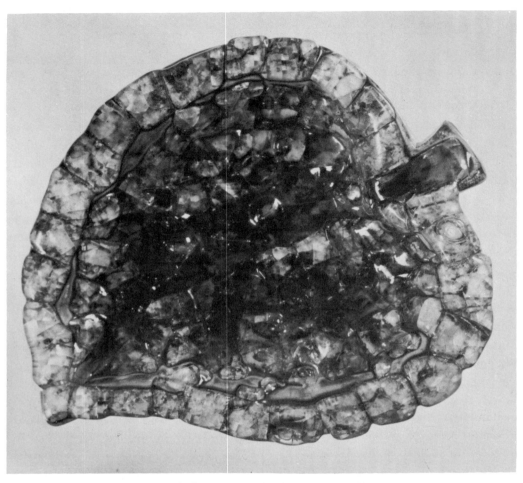

Fig. 287. Glass shards on ceramic bisque. (Work of Florence Mallow.)

Since the individual glass shards comprise an over-all pattern in themselves, additional design would be rather superfluous. While the spotting of color to create a mosaic effect might be effective on a glass base, any of the definite design techniques tend to be distracting and to nullify the three-dimensional quality of the superimposed glass. Usually a light wash of any transparent color (or colors) for glass is sufficient to accent the depth of the glass against the opaque background of the bisque. As illustrated in the foregoing section on clay grilles, the glass glaze colors both glass and clay, while aiding in the fusion between the two.

You have noted that glass assumes different forms at various firing temperatures (Cycle of Glass Subjected to Heat). For this project, sheathing the bisque without individual separation of the glass is the objective, and consequently firing should be terminated before the jeweling stage is reached. Depending on the atmosphere of the kiln and the protective depth of the bisque shape, the correct temperature will be from 1400° to 1450°F.

154

G. GLASS AND METAL

As pointed out in an earlier section, glass has a tendency to release or partially release from metals. This characteristic is substantiated by the fact that when bare copper wire is used to indent glass, the wire design releases after firing. The reference pertained to a technique where the glass area was greater than the wire design, and contact with the wire was minimal. However, it is not merely a matter of minimal contact. Those who are familiar with the enameling of metals know that pure glass forms release from unenameled surfaces, and that a coat of enamel is a prerequisite for the adhesion of glass. Metal frames or shapes, therefore, can be prepared to receive glass as an adjunct to enameling. Since our main concern is the glass itself with the metal an accessory, so to speak, we searched for a basic principle to apply to any project combining the two materials. We had only to evaluate the field of metals in a broader sense to find such a principle. Before metals (other than copper) can be enameled, they must be prepared to assure cohesion with the enamel. Research indicated that the usual agent was a coating of some cobalt-bearing material. Cobalt is a powerful flux, and it seems apparent that it was the factor which brought to-

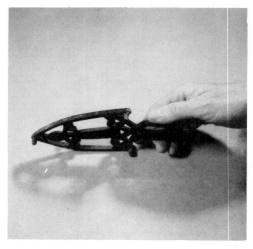

Fig. 288. The trivet has "legs"; glass crushings could not be contained within the openings.

Fig. 289. The legs are pressed into soft firebrick, indicating position.

Fig. 290. Holes are then drilled in the firebrick.

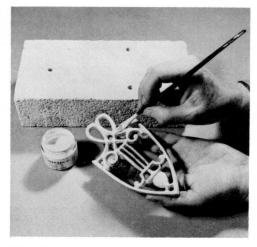

Fig. 291. The trivet is coated with cobalt-bearing glass glaze . . .

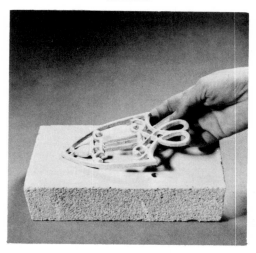

Fig. 292. . . . and placed on the brick, which has been coated with separator. The legs are sunk into the holes.

Fig. 293. The openings are filled with various colors of crushed glass. The fired glass glaze gives a gunmetal sheen on cast iron.

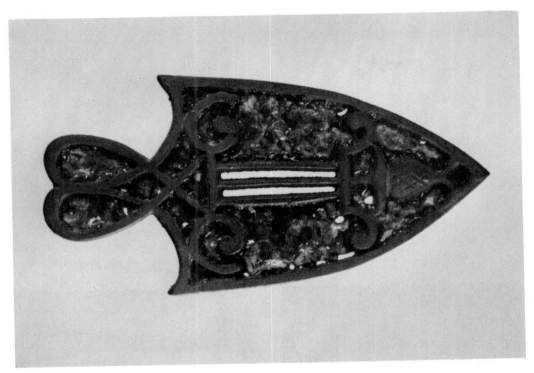

Fig. 294. The finished trivet, after firing.

gether two dissimilar materials. Experimentation revealed that any cobalt and flux combination which would melt at a temperature compatible with the fusion of glass would be effective as a common denominator, thus eliminating an extra treatment. From a practical standpoint, this indicated one of the "glass glazes," which has proved satisfactory so far, with the combinations tested: the cast-iron trivet, the welded-steel frame, and the glass-contained wire enclosure. For obvious reasons, the glass used in these combination techniques was in the form of crushings.

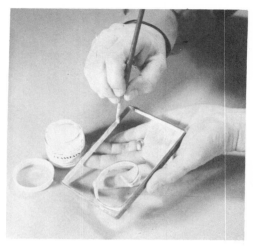

Fig. 295. The inner walls of the frame are coated with cobalt glass glaze.

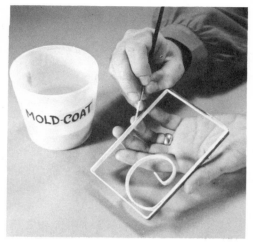

Fig. 296. To prevent fire scale from attracting to the glass during the firing, the top and outer edges of the frame are coated with separator.

Fig. 297. Thin plastic is taped to the kiln shelf . . .

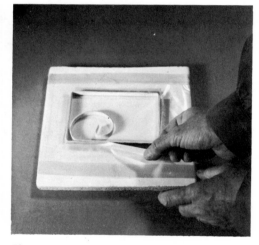

Fig. 298. . . . the frame is taped to the plastic . . .

Fig. 299. . . . and the frame is filled with colored crushed glass. The colors are blended by overlapping spoonfuls. Crushings are occasionally tamped, especially at corners.

Fig. 300. The fired project. Frame has become a stained glass "window."

H. GLASS AND PUMICE

Although still in the experimental stage, the combination of glass and pumice seems promising.

Pumice has been described or defined as being "light, spongy volcanic rock; a volcanic form of natural foam glass." It could well be either or both of these, depending on the geographical source. All definitions agree that pumice is used extensively in scouring powders and other abrasive cleaning products. That it appears in diverse formations is evident from personal observation; I have viewed black, somewhat glossy specimens with very sharp points, as well as the more usual softer, gray-veined structure.

Lightweight and quite easy to carve, the gray pumice did not seem to contain any natural silica, and no fusion to the glass could be perceived after the first firing of the two. The addition of a coating of glass glaze served to bond the two on a subsequent firing.

More attention to detailed carving of the pumice will follow advanced possibilities of fluxing agents.

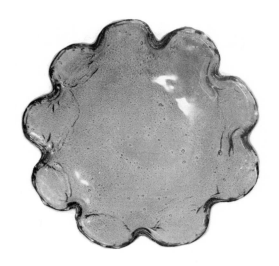

I. GLASS CLINIC

This is a list of questions most frequently asked, and the answers to them. For the most part, indifferent results in bending glass can be attributed to a lack of understanding of the techniques used in firing. The most outstanding craftsmanship in decorating glass can be completely nullified by overfiring or underfiring. I sincerely hope that the following definitions will serve as guides to those experimenting with the fusion of glass for the first time.

Balloons (Unplanned Bubbles of Varying Sizes)

1. Usually Too Fast a Firing. The kiln, depending on size, should be vented, by propping the door or lid open ½", for a longer period (from 15 minutes to one hour). When an 022 cone tips, it is safe to close the door or lid. This applies to glass fired on a kiln shelf as well as on molds. Because they are exposed to even heat, flat panels should be fired 50°F. less than bent pieces would be fired.

2. Prolonged Firing. Although the glass blank may bend perfectly, heating past the bending temperature causes the glass to start another action as a mass, sometimes an entire section folding over, or upwards. This is usually accompanied by numerous needlepoints on edges, and the receding of any surface colorant.

Fig. 301. A bubble on a flat panel, caused by too fast a firing.

3. *Unvented Molds.* If the expanding air in the mold cavity cannot escape through the modeling of the mold, such as fluting or cigarette rests, the pressure causes bubbles to form. On flat-rimmed molds, tiny holes can be drilled in the mold, approximately halfway between the top and the bottom. The air can thus be expelled by the sagging blank.

4. *Height of the Shelf Above.* Although cone or pyrometer readings may indicate correct kiln temperature, a shelf positioned directly over the mold and blank deflects additional heat. Always set an upper shelf at least four inches above the top of the glass blank.

5. *Overloaded Kiln.* Attempts to crowd many molds on shelves create a hotter kiln atmosphere. Molds retain additional heat. Always allow ample space for the circulation of air around molds.

6. *Lamination.* Excessive oil or pigments sandwiched between two layers of glass. Edges of the blanks sometimes fuse before organic matter is burned out, and the expanding air cannot escape. Often accompanied by discoloration of decorating materials.

Areas entirely enclosed by wire in flat panels prevent the escape of air above the level of the wire on which the upper blank rests. Never completely enclose a wire design on the lower blank.

Fracturing

1. *Too Rapid Heating of the Kiln.* Usually occurs in the 500°F. to 700°F. range. Remedy: slower rise in temperature, as indicated in 1. Balloons (above).

2. *Too Sudden Cooling.* Usually occurs in the 850°F. down to 500°F. range. It is the nature of glass to expand under heat and to contract while cooling, and neither process can be hurried.

3. *Irregularities in Cutting the Glass Blank Often Start an Invisible Fracture Which Develops During the Firing.* Check the edges of the blank for minute score lines deviating from the general shape.

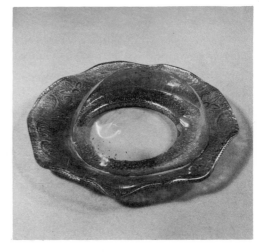

Fig. 302. A bubble in a bent bowl, caused by prolonged firing.

4. Lamination. Two or more different thicknesses of glass. Varying thicknesses (or different brands of glass of equal thickness) expand and contract differently. Always use the same brand and thickness of glass for lamination. If possible, cut both blanks from the same sheet of glass.

5. Adherence to the Mold. Blanks which extend beyond the mold even slightly, tend to soften and curl over the side. Insufficient whiting or other mold separator may allow the blank to attach itself to the mold. Bound to the mold, the blank cannot sag evenly, and fracturing occurs when the free portions of the blank slump.

6. Unequal Placement or Size of Decorative Solids, such as jewels, crushed glass areas, etc., on the surface or when laminated. Too great a variance in weight of extra materials impedes the free action of the bending blank or blanks. Distribute such additions fairly evenly.

7. Lamination of Metal Screen, Wire, Etc. Metals, unless of fine composition, are rigid and will not sag or stretch with the glass. Use metals only in laminating flat panels requiring no movement of the glass blanks. Sections of sheet metals which are too large can fracture laminated glass panels. The upper blank must form over the metal sections, while the lower blank remains as originally placed. Thus, only half of the glass unit moves, resulting in strain. Keep the size of metals subordinate to the area of glass.

8. Re-bending. Glass, as a material, expands when heated. When the bent piece is refired, it cannot expand;

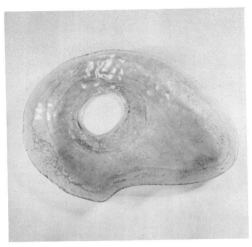

Fig. 303. A bubble in a bent bowl, caused by extreme overfiring. The bubble burst during the firing, and subsequently the sharp edges healed and rounded, starting the cycle of thermal reaction again.

pressure against the rigid mold results in fracture unless the mold is gently sloping.

Frosting or Discoloration

1. Insufficient Venting of the Kiln. See Balloons (above).

2. Condensation. Moisture in the kiln condenses, affecting the gloss of the blank. Always dry applied colorants before firing, and check the condition of mold separators. Dry separators can absorb moisture from the air during damp weather. If the separator is dense, heavy, or difficult to sift, dry the mold before firing. Separators in liquid form give off steam if fired immediately. Always dry the mold 24 to 36 hours in a warm room, if the separator is sprayed or painted on the mold.

3. Fumes. Dried overglazes (china paints), metallic overglazes (liquid gold, palladium, etc.), and lusters emit

163

fumes during the initial stages of firing (up to cone 022). Preburn these materials past the smoking period, or stack them on an upper shelf, to prevent fumes from coming in contact with other glass blanks.

4. Introduction of Combustible Material. Plastics, sequins, cereals, etc. burn out, giving off fumes. Use only materials that are designed for firing.

5. Stained Glass. Certain brands and colors of stained glass contain ingredients which undergo chemical change in firing. Always test-fire small sections of unfamiliar stained glass. If dulling of the surface occurs consistently, some types respond to a thin application of jeweling flux, mixed with water and applied with a brush.

Disfiguration of the Subsurface

The bottom of a bent blank can show an unpleasant appearance, ranging from opaque dullness to actual encrustation. This indicates a conflict between the glass and the mold separator, and a chemical change.

1. Condensation; Dampness of Whiting or Other Separator. Whiting is a chemical known as calcium carbonate; it will undergo a change to calcium oxide when heated. Moisture further effects a chemical change. Be sure that whiting is dry before firing. See paragraph 2. under "Frosting or Discoloration," above.

2. Adherence of Separator. Oil from the skin attracts whiting to the glass and also effects a chemical change in the whiting. Handle the blank only by the edges. If possible, clean the subsurface of the blank with alcohol solvent just before placement of the whiting.

3. Re-use of Separator. Re-use of whiting invariably produces dulling of the subsurface. Firing destroys the qualities of the carbonate form. Always use fresh whiting for each firing.

4. Stained Glass. See under Frosting or Discoloration.

5. Uncleaned Subsurfaces. Any surface decorating materials which become fluid during the firing are also fluid on the subsurfaces, and combine with whiting to form a crust. Subsurfaces and vertical edges of the blank should be checked, and cleaned of colorant traces.

J. SUMMARY

Within these few pages, I have introduced you to one of the most fascinating crafts available to the average person. Requiring a minimum expenditure for equipment and materials, working with glass affords a glimpse into what seems a veritable miracle of change through physical manipulation, introduction of chemicals, and application of heat.

There has been little direction toward definite projects, for the techniques can be applied to diverse finished articles, according to the imagination of the designer.

The educator may work with glass to illustrate clearly many principles of chemistry, physics, and elementary science. In art departments, glass can be used to pinpoint color and design when light is transmitted or reflected, and values of color contrast and of shading may be projected on a screen, or studied at close hand. Glass craft can be taught in ceramic departments, and illustrative courses incorporating glass are often given as an aid to preliminary instruction in silk-screening, watercolor, architecture, and commercial art. Except in mental institutions, where glass is considered of possible danger to patients, glass and its properties have proved to be of considerable value to other related subjects.

The creative homemaker, seeking a

specific bowl for flower arrangements, an unusual lamp, or even a complete set of dishes, may become interested in the extensive use of glass in building a new home or remodeling a present residence.

Although the procedures outlined in this book are not those of the commercial factory, the basic principles remain the same except that hand labor is used. The craftsman can readily find a market for his wares with the interior decorator or in shops which feature custom work.

Whether your goal is to earn a living, to teach, or to express individual creativity, you will certainly derive great personal satisfaction from this new art experience. Undoubtedly many of you will delve more deeply into the technical aspects, and evolve new variations of basic procedures, or perhaps accidentally discover new ways of manipulation, new forms or substances, new pigments which have an affinity for glass. Others of you will accept and use the suggestions as they are literally given. To all, I extend sincere encouragement in the ever-growing field of artistic endeavor.

GLOSSARY

Alumina hydrate: A fine white powder used as a separator between glass and mold (or kiln shelf).

Anneal: The tempering of glass by slow and gradual cooling (sometimes used in reference to thermal shock treatment of glass: heat followed by water quenching, to weaken the structure prior to crushing).

Asbestos: Fibers obtained from chrysotile, a hydrated magnesium silicate rock. Asbestos is fireproof.

Atmosphere: The kind of air prevailing in any place, as within a kiln during firing.

Bat: A flat slab of material, usually plaster; used as a base for construction of clay forms.

Bent: Sheet glass shaped into three-dimensional form by firing on, within, or over clay or metal forms. Syn.: Sagged.

Blank: A piece of glass cut to pattern or predetermined measurements, for a specific use.

Bond: To adhere glass (or other materials) to glass by means of firing.

Calcine: To make powdery through action of dry heat.

Calcium carbonate (whiting): A finely ground white powder, used as a separator in glass firing.

Carborundum: Carbide of silicon; an extremely hard abrasive.

Chuck: A contrivance for holding a tool or drill bit.

Cleavage: Severance of glass; usually the final separation resulting from scoring with a glass cutter.

Coefficient: A number indicating degree of change, as in expansion and contraction.

Cohesion: The state or act of sticking together.

167

Cone: Elongated triangle form; used to indicate heat penetration during firing of a kiln.

Corrosion: The process of being worn or eaten away, as in oxidation of metals through chemicals and/or heat.

Enamel: A smooth, tough substance used in coating surfaces of glass or metal. Usually supplied in dry powder form.

Flux: A prepared, low melting glass, usually colorless, which may be mixed with pigments to produce vitrifiable coatings on glass.

Formulate: To reduce to or express in a formula; to state definitely.

Fracture: To break or crack.

Fragmentation: Sections or shards of glass fired together.

Frit: A glassy material, usually in granular form, produced by fusing a mixture of some or all of the constituents of a glaze or enamel so as to render insoluble any soluble materials present and also to insure greater homogeneity; to lower the melting point, and to render toxic compounds nonpoisonous.

Fuse: To liquefy by means of heat; to melt.

Glass: A hard, brittle substance, usually transparent, formed by fusing silica, an alkali, and some other base.

Glaze: A vitreous coating.

Grog: Fired clay, firebrick, quartz, etc., which has been ground up and screened. It may be added to clay to allow moisture to escape, and thus reduce cracking and warping.

Impervious: Impenetrable.

Incise: To cut lines or characters into the surface of; to engrave.

Infrared: Denoting rays outside the red end of the spectrum; employed as a means of drying inner as well as surface structures.

Kiln: An oven in which things are dried, hardened or vitrified.

Laminate: To construct of successive layers.

Linear: Composed of lines.

Luster (lustre): A solution of mineral pigments in a suitable organic solvent. The pigments are either precious metals or tinctorial oxides of certain base metals. Lusters are applied by brushing or spraying. Upon firing, they leave behind an extremely thin layer of metal oxides which are fused into the glass.

Metallic overglaze: As above; higher percentage of metal content. Firing results in discernible platings.

Mica: A mineral silicate that forms into thin transparent leaves. Mica flakes, when laminated, impart a bubbled texture within a fused glass piece.

Mold: A hollow form which determines contour of a glass blank fired upon it.

Overglaze: A low-firing pigment requiring a glossy surface as a base coating.

Oxide: A compound of oxygen and a base substance or compound.

Oxidize: To combine with oxygen.

Parallax: The seeming displacement of an object by reason of a change in the observer's position.

Parallel: One of two or more equidistant lines or planes.

Perimeter: The outer boundary of any plane figure.

Project: Specific plan or design utilizing one or more techniques of manipulation or decoration.

Pyrometer: An instrument to measure high degrees of heat.

Refractory: Resisting the action of heat.

Rheostat: An instrument regulating the strength of an electric current by controlling the amount of resistance.

Sagged: *see* Bent.

Score: To mark with grooves, usually with a cutter or tool designed for the purpose.

Segment: A separated part; an individual piece.

Shard: A fragment of broken glass or clay.

Silica: A raw material used in manufacturing glass; usually supplying the glossy or vitreous constituent.

Silicate of Soda (sodium silicate): "Water glass"; sometimes used as an adhesive.

Strata: Two or more layers.

Subsurface: The underside of a glass blank or sheet of glass.

Superimpose: To place one thing upon another.

Surface: The outer face of a solid body; usually the upper level of a sheet of glass.

Technique: The manner of handling details in the execution of an undertaking.

Terra cotta: A composition of unfired and finely ground fire clay.

Texture: Discernible uneven surfaces.

Thermal: Pertaining to heat.

Translucent: Partial transmitting of light; objects beyond translucent substances are not distinguishable.

Transparent: Permitting the passage of light so that objects may be seen.

Underglaze: An opaque colorant requiring glaze or glass as a surface coating.

Vent: To allow escape of air or fumes through an opening; an opening or aperture which will permit passage of air or fumes.

Viscous: Adhesive; sticky.

Vitreous: Consisting of or resembling glass.

Vitrified: Converted into glass.

Volatile: Tending to turn into vapor; easily changed into gas.

Whiting: *see* Calcium carbonate.

APPENDIX

Note: Since many packaging firms release materials under their own names, manufacturers of some materials and equipment are unknown outside of certain areas; the author can therefore recommend only such materials and equipment as have been received. There are doubtless identical or similar products issued under other brand names.

The following list is comprised of materials which have been tested in the California laboratories:

CERAMIC MATERIALS:

Flux: Drakenfeld Co.; Ferro Corp.; O. Hommel Co.; Vitro

Frits: Ferro Corp.; Glostex; O. Hommel Co.; Pemco

Stained glass flux: Kay Kinney Contoured Glass

Terra-cotta clay: Sewer pipe manufacturers; Suppliers of modeling clay

COLORANTS:

"Glasstain" (*glass glaze*): Kay Kinney Contoured Glass

Metallic overglaze; Lusters: Dupont; Englehardt Co. (Hanovia Div.); O. Hommel Co.

Overglaze: Reward Co.; Zirco

Translucent ceramic underglaze: Duncan Ceramic Supplies; Reward Co.

GLASS:

Chunk flint: Kay Kinney Contoured Glass

Novelty (bracelets): India Imports; Albert J. Kessler. Co.

Solar: Pittsburgh Glass Co.

Stained (cathedral): Blenko Glass Co.; Kokomo Opalescent Glass Co.

Textured: Mississippi Glass Co.

Window: Libbey-Owens-Ford

HAND TOOLS:

Bits (prismatic and spade drill): Somers & Mach Co.

Brushes: Delta; Holbein; Marx

Glass cutters (circle, gauge, hand, and lens): Fletcher-Terry Co.

KILNS:

J. J. Cress Co.

RUBBER ABRASIVE WHEELS:

Cratex

SEPARATORS:

Alumina hydrate: Ferro Corp.; O. Hommel Co.

Mold coat: Kay Kinney Contoured Glass

Whiting (calcium carbonate, ceramic grade): Ferro Corp.; O. Hommel Co.

SPRAYERS:

Jet-Pak; Paasche; Pee-Wee; Wold

TOOLS:

Disposal: Waste King Co.

Drill press: Sears, Roebuck & Co.

MISCELLANEOUS:

Alcohol solvent (denatured alcohol): Paint suppliers

Calcined gold mica: Kay Kinney Contoured Glass

Enamels: Thomas Thompson Co.

Fiberglass: Drapery and yardage firms; marine suppliers

Graphite (glass) pencils: Kay Kinney Contoured Glass

Metal foils: Thomas Thompson Co.

Mica: Building suppliers; insulation

Nichrome wire: Electrical suppliers

Sodium bisulphate: Garden and nursery suppliers; Sparex

INDEX